As an evolutionary explorer, I encounter every now and then
another kindred person on the same path who possesses a
brilliance and deep understanding of our evolutionary potential.
Alan Sasha Lithman is such a person. I highly recommend his
Evolutionary Agenda to all those who feel the emergent
potential of humanity arising in their hearts, and who
long to be more effective in their actions in the world.
**Barbara Marx Hubbard, President, Foundation for Conscious
Evolution; author of *Emergence* and *Conscious Evolution***

An
Evolutionary
Agenda

For the Third Millennium

To Larry —
For the Journey...

Onward!

Sasha

10-17-04

An
Evolutionary
Agenda

For the Third Millennium

A Primer for the
Mutation of Consciousness

ALAN SASHA LITHMAN

WHITE CLOUD PRESS
Ashland, Oregon

Printed in Malaysia

First White Cloud Press edition: 2003

Cover design: David Rupee, Impact Publications

ISBN 1-883991-54-4

To Sri Aurobindo,
who led me to the well

To the Divine Mother,
wellspring of Grace

To the Earth,
healed of our blindness and abuse

CONTENTS

ONE

INTRODUCTION
THE EVOLUTION OF CONSCIOUSNESS

Placing the Evolutionary Fine Print Up-Front

To understand where we're heading, we must first find our true footing. Where exactly *are* we standing? In which time? On what ground? And who or what exactly is this "we"?

In fact, beginning literally where we are, what is this page we are reading and how did these words and thoughts manifest on it? Is it, as our outer senses tell us, processed plant matter which grew at some definable point in time in a particular bioregion of earth, now technologically transformed into paper imprinted with someone's ideas formulated in English? Or is it recycled molecular material, spun from the original protoplasm of an embryonic Universe whose genes, coded with the DNA of Consciousness, date back to that unrecorded moment when Matter and Time, according to our mind's grasp of Reality, began? Is it a tangible sheet of text, white with black script, whose words remain constant no matter how many times one closes and reopens the book? Or is it a whirling mass of micro-worlds, of electrons spinning at such imperceptible lightspeeds as to appear motionless and stable, energy held together in discrete forms—in this case, a printed page—by a remarkable force of physics?

Or is it all of the above, depending on which dimension, which layer of consciousness we operate, perceive and translate our reality?

An innocuous piece of paper or a symbol of the miraculous containing the secret code of Being? Held together by a force of physics? *meta*physics? or simply a Force of Consciousness still slipping through the hands of physicists and others who do not yet have the inner instruments to recognize that they too are held together and *in*-formed by this same conscious Force, that we too are an evolving expression of that same emergent Consciousness?—of a conscious Presence, Self-born, Self-conceived, who in the metaphoric flash of a smile, once upon a time, once upon eternity, went supernova, kindling Being into Becoming, primal stardust sown into spiraling galaxies pregnant with planetary seeds: seeds of self ingrained in stone, crystallizing into atoms, clustering into molecules, coalescing finally into an earth whose vulcan crust still held that timeless creative Star-Fire until it could hold it no more...

...That Fire breaking forth through its womb of Matter, spilling forth in a myriad forms of Life, cells quickening, dancing, blazing forth in a sea of grasses and flowering plants, celebrating from the cellular and photosynthetic through the spectrum of the four-legged and finally the two; crossing another evolutionary threshold from Life to Mind, forging from the primordial matrix of these living elements a new form for that first Fire to speak and know Itself, reconfiguring these living elements, churning the alchemy from one-celled plants to protozoa to primates to people so that people could turn plants into pages, into stories, into music, into works of art and ideas reflecting the joy and wonder of that original Creative Fire hidden in every moment, every act, every breath, every birth.

Language cultures the way we process and translate Reality. Human language, though capable of leaps, is still an awkward and approximate means of communication. Gender-divisive and gender-biased, strung out piece-meal in linear phrases of either-or, black or white, replete with blindspots and obscurities that correspond to the limits of our own present level of human consciousness, language, like us, is still in its "rough-draft" stage of development, too opaque and compartmentalized for transparent and direct transmission of experience.

Indicative of our blindspots, we have, for the most part, grown accustomed to the inherent limitations and biases of our languages, turning their flaws and distortions into norms, accepting them — as we accept ourselves — without questioning the implications of those distorted norms, without recognizing that these evolving forms of communication and consciousness reduce Reality to their own terms, their own intermediary levels. In other words, in the very attempt to grasp Reality, to seize the meaning of our selves, we get in our own way. We eclipse or, at best, obscure the light, fixating on the shadow our ego casts: on forms projected through varying degrees and lenses of unconsciousness or partial consciousness, defined through still-evolving sensory and cognitive filters that overlay Reality, translating It through themselves rather than the other way round.

Operating through these blinders whose self-deceptive nature also keeps us from becoming aware that we are wearing them grants them a powerful sacrosanctity, deflecting our questions and doubts, turning them outward, preventing us from getting too close to calling the bluff of an enormous ignorance that controls not only our knowledge but our *way* of knowing—that fundamentally prejudices and conditions our orientation to what is real, establishing the *way* we look at things without ever questioning the framework that filters what we see.

And if our subject matter is an inquiry into the very nature of that Reality, into the evolution of Consciousness itself, then we must be prepared to humbly question everything: *all* of our premises, assumptions and self-concepts, no matter how sacred, not just probing *what* we know but *how* we know. In which case, this work is not only an attempt to penetrate the present threshold of our consciousness as a species, but a struggle, particularly at the outset, to formulate this attempt within the existing ego-embedded structure of human language, running against the grain of its predominant male-mind mechanics, accents, dialects and dialectics.

With this understanding, I ask the reader to bear with me if the writing occasionally grafts in hybrid words or slips from essay-style prose into metaphoric imagery and symbolism more akin to poetry or myth. For this Thesis not only concerns itself with the rational attempt to comment upon its subject matter but, to the extent possible, to *enter* it, especially if one intends to propose an evolutionary agenda for our species based upon it.

In this context, then, visionary symbols and script are incorporated not so much as devices to prove or explain but rather to catch and convey something of the experience itself — like a mantra that convinces not through a secondary process of analytical reasoning, but simply because it rings true, self-evident, resonating with and awakening a corresponding truth in us, speaking directly to a core self and deeper sense in us. As such, these creative, more fluid applications of language, though riskier for those of us accustomed to more externally verifiable means of expression, are better adapted to evoke, expand and explore the unprecedented, inviting something wider and freer to breathe into them and us: to *inspire*, bypassing the defensive illogic of a mind programmed to reject that which it does not already know or, more threatening, that which it does not know *how* to know, challenging the supremacy of Mind and mental knowing, opening the possibility of another way to know and be.

With Consciousness as the subject of our inquiry, we are, reader and writer alike, not merely detached observers but intimately, inseparably and subjectively involved in our subject matter. It is both unrealistic and unreasonable, then, for us to hold this inquiry up to some artificial standard of objectivity and proof or to expect that we will emerge from such a process untouched and unchanged ourselves. This recognition is not intended to excuse or exempt this work from accountability for its proposals, premises and hypotheses. It is simply a statement of fact which places the awesome responsibility for testing the veracity of things back upon ourselves, *each* of us, encouraging us to reclaim our reference point in the equation, recovering a core common sense which reminds us that just because we cannot prove an experience does not disprove it either. Proof may simply lie in another level of consciousness than that presently available to the seeker or his/her instruments of inquiry.

This work, then, proposes to explore the evolution of Consciousness in a way that is both visionary yet common-sensible, based on the following premises:

- Only that which is already *in*-volved can *e*-volve.
- Evolution proceeds simultaneously on two interwoven tracks, one of form, the other of consciousness.
- Form is essentially a construct, vehicle or vessel (in Sanskrit, *adhar*) of consciousness, a medium through which consciousness expresses and experiences itself.
- *Human* being represents a particular stage in the evolving spectrum of *conscious* Being, a threshold of consciousness corresponding to a particular range of mental frequency or bandwidth in an infinite scale of Being.
- Humanity is both a distinct form and frequency of consciousness as well as a unique metamorphic species, an evolutionary work-in-progress, whose essential destiny and *dharma*[1] is to consciously exceed itself: a transitional

---

1. The Sanskrit term "dharma" refers to the self-law, inner destiny or archetypal truth of one's being. This *dharma*, at once unique to each individual as well as generic when applied at the collective or prototypal level, corresponds to the Greek *entelécheia*.

"bridging" species whose upper threshold of consciousness, despite formidable guardians of that threshold, can be self-bridged and surpassed in a transformational process that progressively leads to a new terrestrial species, emerging like our amphibious ancestors into a new milieu of consciousness.

- We exist in two overlapping times, historical and evolutionary, one a sub-rhythm of the other.
- We are at a transitional moment when the cresting wave of an evolutionary cycle overtakes history's shallower process and perspective, pressing us against our upper threshold as a species, sweeping us in the inrushing evolutionary tide toward a new principle of Being.
- In the course of this transition, fraught with species-level labor pains, we are pushed to the brink of our own mutation by the accelerating intensity of inner and outer crises — a catalyst of crises which, like a psy-particle accelerator splitting the atom of our ego, continues to bombard the dense cocoon of all that remains unconscious in us, facing us with the perilous choice of transformation or extinction.
- Our primary focus as a species at this crucial evolutionary turning-point is to learn to collaborate more consciously, gracefully and co-creatively with the dynamics of this change; to learn *to breathe*, working *with* the contractions, minimizing the frictions and traumas of the transition.

An Applied Evolutionary Research

The challenge set forth in this introduction lies in developing, elaborating and illustrating these premises, grounding them in the context of present reality rather than leaving them hanging as abstract concepts. For the intent of this evolutionary agenda is not only to provide a more coherent and clarifying perspective—a more embracing and integrating framework to focus and make sense of the often-chaotic and overwhelming intensity of terrestrial events/ crises—but to suggest and explore practical ways to apply this emerging perception in our individual and societal evolution. In other words, moving our inquiry into the nature of Consciousness from theoretical to applied research, risking to innovate and adapt creative strategies that translate what we discover into actions, not just ideas or insights, empowering ourselves as a species to intervene in our evolutionary destiny rather than passively submitting as victims to the consequences of our present course and its flat-world wisdom.

If, as this work suggests, we are a transitional species at an evolutionary turning-point, then our crises take on new meaning. Behind their terrifying masks, they are the catalysts, levers and agents of our change, the response of an interactive Reality mirroring back to us all that needs to change within ourselves. And as such, despite the specter they cast over our future, their real threat is to the authority of our past, prodding us forward, overcoming our reluctance to evolve by ratcheting up the pain—a crude but essential evolutionary mechanism to keep us from getting too comfortable with who, what and where we have been, seduced by our gravity— until we have learned to replace the need for pain with a more conscious and effective will-to-evolve.

Solutions, then, that default to the past for answers or that rely on the complex variations of denial and escape, mundane or mystic, we have devised or discovered over the millennia, are only half-truths that miss both the evolutionary point and turning-point. Consciously facing and entering the core of our crises, intimidating as that may be, remains the challenge for those who truly seek to resolve them.

In this light, self-evolution is not a glorified spiritual escape mechanism: A cut-and-run transcendence (our patriarchal problem-solving reflex) to some etheric or disembodied state that conveniently disconnects us from the torments and frustrations of earth-life, effectively condemning terrestrial reality to an inherently inferior, sinful, futile, absurd or illusory existence. It is rather the other direction: A healing and wholing, a more conscious and compassionate entering into, expanding one's identity and capacity to identify with; and in that process, becoming and fulfilling who and what one truly is, not only reclaiming and transforming our selves but reaffirming Matter, re-experiencing our true context and creative relationship with Her and terrestrial reality, redefining "holy" by what is whole.

Onward then into our self-bridging, into this applied evolutionary research which the eternal child-explorer in us knows simply as "the Adventure of Consciousness"[2]....

---

2. The phrase "adventure of consciousness" has its origins in Sri Aurobindo's epic poem *Savitri*. A turning-point influence and experience in my life, Sri Aurobindo was at once a poet, revolutionary, visionary thinker and yogi. Following his return to India from his Cambridge-educated period in England at the end of the Nineteenth Century, he shifted existential gears and focus; moving from the forefront of the Indian Freedom Struggle and the sphere of cultural and political change into a far more subversive activism; fronting the very root-change and transformation of human consciousness itself.

In describing himself and his work, Sri Aurobindo once remarked: "...It is not with the Empyrean that I am busy: I wish it were. It is rather with the opposite end of things..." From the late 1800s until his passing in 1950, he uncompromisingly pursued this transformational goal; transcribing, editing and updating his vision and experience in the process through more than thirty volumes of collected works; infusing terms and concepts such as "evolution of consciousness", "integral yoga" and "integration" into the genepool of human vocabulary long before the advent of the human potentials movement or the emergent fields of transpersonal psychology and holistic healing; anonymously cross-pollinating East and West a generation before American bookstores began to fill their shelves with best-selling gurus and mystic texts.

TWO

THE DNA OF CONSCIOUSNESS

Evolution as a field of scientific research is still more a description of a phenomenon rather than an explanation of it: An increasingly refined graph of the observable universe's unfolding, meticulously piecing together the emerging Story—the molecular, cellular and neuro-chemical chain of events that brought us, the still-evolving inquirers in this Inquiry, into being. Science's remarkable version of events, however, which in the accelerating span of a few brief centuries has pressed back through some 13.7 billion years (at present rough estimates) to the event phenomenon itself of a nascent universe, still remains, like us, a work-in-progress, conceding significant missing links: How *did* life emerge from apparently insensate and inorganic matter? How *did* mind emerge from apparently insentient and unconscious matter? And preceding these, how did matter itself emerge from apparent nothingness? And *why*? What, if any, is the intention and direction?

For our credentialed religions, on the other hand, whether theistic or non-theistic, the very concept of evolution remains anathema or enigma, leading us to another set of unasked or unanswered questions that tug embarrassingly at the cloak of their authority.

Evolution and Revolution

Evolution, while primarily associated with incremental changes over immeasurably vast periods of time, is in fact a far more subversive, radical and transformative process than its revolutionary human spin-offs. For if one strips away the associative meanings and hyperbole, revolution suggests a circular movement rotating around a fixed axis that, regardless of the distance traveled, eventually returns to the orbital point where it began. This is why there is a tendency, a gravitational pull in our human cycles, for revolutionaries, once in power, to take on the qualities of those whom they overthrew—to gravitate back to past patterns, the oppressed and abused unconsciously absorbing and repeating the tyrannies of their oppressors and abusers.

The central element here that limits the effectiveness of revolutionary change is its rotation around a fixed axis, which in human terms means around a fixed consciousness. In other words, if the person, the inner consciousness, the pivotal point, does not change, shift, *evolve*, then things simply *re*volve, tethered in the case of our species to Mind and its mental reference points for Reality. The changes, then, which that circumscribed consciousness brings about remain temporal, superficial, limited in scope and degree: System-makeovers which do not reach the core person, core programming, eventually returning us to a variation of the previously-existing regime, a variation of ourselves and all that remains, despite appearances, untransformed in us.

Evolution, on the other hand, resembles a spiral movement rather than a closed circle. Its fractal symbol of itself can be seen in the spiraling double-helix of the DNA molecule, evolution's mercurial messenger and the truly subversive double-agent of Change. Its serpentine image of intertwining strands conveys both

- a corkscrew pressure to penetrate, to break through stasis and status quo not only at the surface but at the center, the nucleus, the core of the form, shifting the axis of consciousness to another level, another dimension; as well as
- interlinking threads that weave together and reintegrate the breakthroughs, inner and outer movements, ascending and descending directions, bridging the disconnections be-

tween form and consciousness in one vast continuum of Being.

As an archetypal symbol, the molecular structure and function of DNA remarkably mirrors the coiled *Kundalini*, the Serpent Force and Fire of India's tantras, which, when awakened, threads the axis of Consciousness, breaking through and bridging the polarities of Matter and Spirit.

ട

Evolution, then, and the persistent thrust of its evolutionary movement is a direct threat to all fixed forms, ideas, answers, truths. In which case, those systems and belief systems, whether cellular, psychological, corporate or cultural, which cling to present form, present control, present truth, no matter how true that truth had been in its moment, carry within themselves the seeds of their own stagnation, self-undoing and eventual death. In other words, when the ego[1] of the form fixes and crystallizes, closing its borders, mind or cell-walls to new life, inspiration and ideas, that form begins to collapse in upon itself weighed down by its own gravity, inertia, entropy.

Religions, particularly the more formalized and codified traditions, are no exception. Behind the rhetoric and the robes, they too have their egos, chauvinistic or sublime, even those which profess the goal of ego-transcendence. Beneath their imposing aura of venerability lies a vulnerability, I believe, which, like a clenched fist, hides the emptiness it actually holds, masking itself in the pretense of power.

---

1. "Ego" in this generic sense simply refers to that initial *individualizing* mechanism which binds and identifies consciousness with form, equating self at whatever level of existence—microbial, human or institutional—with a particular temporal form, temporal personality, investing exclusively in that surrogate self, that discrete identity.

In its subtler and more discreet forms, this assumed power presents itself as aloofness and intimidating superiority, as an esoteric elitism whose sophistries mesmerize or mystify the seeker, warding off or discrediting questions that would point—like the child to the naked Emperor's chagrins—to inconsistencies, missing pieces or premises that simply make no sense. In its more ruthless and virulent forms of denial, this clenched fist has appeared, as we have seen through the shadow-side of our sectarian history with its hardcore cults and hierarchies, through crusades to conquer and convert the infidels: through barbaric persecutions, inquisitions and stakeburnings to protect at all costs the sanctity of *their* Way, *their* Word, *their* Truth; excommunicating diversity of thought and experience; subjugating women, minorities, Nature, Native cultures and the more open-ended feminine principle, all of course in the name of God or the very freedoms they profess to worship and honor, contradictions be damned.

In this sense, religions (most egregiously, those spawned by fickle, vengeful and cruel gods) exhibit the same primitive self-preservational instincts and defense mechanisms as biological organisms; subconsciously invested in the priority of their own survival, perpetuation and dominion despite avowed ideals of tolerance, humility or self-transcendence. I believe this common survival instinct suggests that thought-forms—whether religious or secular—and their constellating systems of thought (ideologies) take on the same personality behaviors and egos as life-forms and life-systems. This analogy, not simply intended metaphorically, proposes that the ego-bias of life-forms to survive translates in mind-forms through the corresponding predisposition to be right: a tendency which strengthens and feeds off itself the more the thought, idea or belief is repeated, repetition creating an ego-gravitational field[2] that attracts adherents, proselytes, politicians and preachers, turning hypotheses and individual insights into dogma and eventually law.

The cardinal sin, the *mortal* sin, the evolutionary serpentine sin, then, in this scenario is simply to question the authority of the script or scripture, to suggest that the last word has not yet been written, copyrighted or patented. A heresy that, like the child questioning the Emperor's new clothes, cuts to the very core of our folly, fallibility and mortality as a species.

All breakthroughs are heretical to that which was broken through. In which case, Evolution is Life's ultimate heresy (or deliverer, depending on which side of the breakthrough one finds oneself), pressing not simply at *what* we know and experience, but *the way* we know and experience. In other words, at the very axis of human consciousness in which all of our traditions and revelations are rooted: An axis of consciousness which, till now, we have equated and identified with Mind.

The gauntlet, then, which Darwin threw down—suggesting that we are part of an evolutionary continuum, most recently descended, God forbid, from apes—challenged and offended more than our religious sensibilities. For if one follows the implications of *The Origin of Species* past its last page, past its interim conclusions, in quest of the living and still-evolving version, there is no reason to believe that evolution arbitrarily stops with us, with this half-baked human species and its half-lit mental consciousness. And it is this subversive implication, I believe, which subconsciously pricks not only the raw nerve of our biblical-based realities but of Mind itself as Reality's final arbiter, intermediary and god, provoking a fundamen-

---

2. This proposition parallels the *morphogenetic* field envisioned by Rupert Sheldrake, which suggests that the habitual repetition of a physical pattern or behavior sets up a "morphic resonance" that in time gathers sufficient momentum and gravity until it "grooves" into the appearance of physical law and inevitability.

*tal*ist backlash which continues to this day in a contagion of forms and cultures, secular as well as sectarian, all desperately resisting that inrushing evolutionary tide that presses us now toward a new principle of Being—toward a mutation of consciousness that threatens not simply our social, political and economic empires but the Empire of Mind itself as evolution's last word.

In this sense, this work aspires to serve not simply as a support and encouragement for original thought and action—for personal, community and environmental activism—but as a catalyst and agent for a more integral and radical *evolutionary* activism, lending itself to that growing wave, that conscious counter-contagion of creative change and discontent churning within and around us. From this perspective, then, let us, like the innocent and irreverent child, explore some of the prejudices, inconsistencies, unasked questions and missing pieces swept under the millennial rug not only by our theistic traditions but by our non-theistic and atheistic traditions as well, sincerely following our Inquiry wherever it may lead us.

Evolution is that troublesome (but pearl-provocative) grain of sand in our cloistered shell, dismissed by biblical creationists as blasphemy; reduced by the more mystical Eastern traditions (which see this material world essentially as *Maya*,[3] Illusion) to another ignorance that foolishly reinvests our attention back into the Illusion rather than into transcending It. In both scenarios, the ultimate, if contradictory, goal of Life is to get out of it, out of the body, not more profoundly into it.

---

3. The Sanskrit term *Maya*, as first expressed in India's Vedas, originally meant that creative, self-comprehending Consciousness which conceives and gives form to the Infinite. Gradually, as human consciousness itself became more divided, this feminine term degraded, taking on the pejorative meaning and association of "Illusion".

The more exoteric Western variations on this theme project us toward some simplistic return to the Father, to heavens beyond this purgatorial and problematic existence left flawed somehow by its Creator. The more sophisticated inner-directed spiritualities orient us toward some transcendent repose, some mystic return to an original, featureless and undivided state of Being, freed from the preoccupation and attachment to this illusory phenomenal world: A realization that liberates us once and for all from this endlessly painful and futile wheel of karma, awakening us like a zen whack on the head from this hypnotic dream-within-a-dream into the (mind-boggling!) enlightenment of one's own material unreality. Carrying this liberation to its ascetic and nihilistic extremes which confuse ego with Self, one does not merely emerge into some egoless transcendent Reality; one throws the baby out with the bathwater, annulling Self and universe as well as ego in some ultimate act of unbeing, like a flame finally extinguished in the recognition that it never really existed.

When one cuts to the core of these creationist, contemplative and nihilistic ideologies, one finds a common negation and denial of Matter, the Fallen Feminine. She is effectively voided of meaning and value, left inexplicably hanging with no relation to Her Self or Source, divorced from what we have ambiguously called "Spirit." So let us begin our probe into the prejudices, inconsistencies and missing pieces with Her.

The Denial of Matter

The denial of Matter, our primogenetic split, is the origin of all our subsequent either-or patterns and dichotomies. Subconsciously implanted in the mythic and paleo-mythic roots of our mind-cultured psyches, it lies there as one of those sacrosanct givens: one of those unhealed assumptions so second-nature that we never in fact even see it, let alone dare to question it. Yet there it is, Matter eternally segregated (if not abandoned altogether) on one side, below;

Spirit luminously above, on the other....leaving Madonna's ultimate Material Girl forever stigmatized, formed somehow from some lesser corporeal (synonymous with non-spiritual), and therefore corruptible, substance; or dismissed outright as an Illusion that never really existed to begin with, mocking not only the words and paper this was written on but the reader and writer as well. But that is *not* what this writer believes nor what these words or paper intend to express.

That which is *suprarational* to our intelligence is not *ir*rational; that which is *supralogical* is not *illogical*. In fact, one would expect a more highly-evolved consciousness to be held up to a higher and clearer standard of sense, not a lower and obscurer one. In which case, faith is not incompatible with common sense ("common" here not implying "ordinary" but a more grounded "unitive," "integrated," "*in*-common" sense that honors rather than denies oneself as a reference point for truth). There is, however, a perverse tendency in us, out of some misplaced notion of loyalty and unworthiness, to blindly and automatically defer to the vibration of authority, even when everything within us, including our own body-sense, revolts, telling us that it is nonsense or madness. Faith unblinded, then, is simply a core intuitive sense in the being that resonates with what rings true, what *feels* real, *commonsensibly* real, even though that truth still remains untranslated or uncertified by mental logic and external methods of proof.

In this light, let us return to the question of Matter.

How, one wonders, is it possible for a Divine Creator to ultimately create something *other* than or outside of Itself? How is it possible to arbitrarily conjure Something from Nothing, fashioned from a substance other than Its own Being? It is far more likely that this split arrangement—God there, mundane world here—simply reflects, describes and projects our own present schizophrenic level of perception. For if there *is* a Divine Being, then there is *only* the Divine. And what we call "Matter" can only be That in various forms, figures and degrees of Consciousness. In other words, Matter *is* the Body of God. In which case, what we call "Evolution" is in fact the progressive manifestation of this Divinity, the unfolding process of an eternal, infinite yet immanent Presence in Its canvass of Time-Space.

Reexamining, then, the motives and logic for this Creation, it is a strange faith indeed which accepts, let alone worships or deifies, a Creator whose sole inspiration is to get out of the Story. Why bother to create something in the first place if the intention is eventually to deny and void it of meaning? Why set up what amounts to an elaborate hoax where the plot and script condemn us to a dead-end experience?—an existential tease where the raison d'être is simply to realize the emptiness of it all, and in that realization, to turn back, frustrated, exhausted, defeated, taking refuge once again in some inner or other transcendent peace and poise where we began? Why, in fact, trade that to begin with for this suffering and illusion, *unless* there is some other sense that we have not yet caught?

For where is the divine logic in some stoic Heavenly Father-figure or disconnected Witness Self masochistically plunging Itself or us into such a painfully unresolvable tale with such a pathetically unimaginative finalé?—a finalé that, if played out to its absurd conclusions, deletes not only the reality of the world but of its Author as well in some last gloriously-mystical *koan* that, like a dream popping and taking the dreamer with it, leaves no trace…. *Unless* we had missed some secret still hidden here in Matter, awaiting another consciousness capable of divining it?—a consciousness for the most part still in the evolutionary wings, capable nevertheless of rewriting the script, breaking the spell of Self-forgetting, awakening the Sleeping Princess, rekindling the coiled Serpent Fire from its cave?

As a writer, it would seem far more plausible that we have simply not yet fathomed the true plot or intention, that we have gotten lost in some of the early sub-plots and intrigues, prematurely judging and underestimating the Author, the Story and ourselves as its evolving characters, as if the narrative was complete, finished rather than still in some interim draft-version. And perhaps it is the very nature of that interim version—that interim mental version with its interim characters that we seem to be acting out—to mistake a stage for the goal, impatiently confusing initial discoveries for ultimate answers, turning interim realizations and revelations into absolute truths; then zealously defending those answers, perceptions and truths regardless of how transparently irrational, conflicted, incomplete or out-dated.

In which case, the Story and its genetic script still remain a Mystery, unfinished and unfulfilled but *not* unfulfillable, waiting for its characters to outgrow their present mental interpretation and rendering of their roles. For if we change the lens of consciousness through which we perceive, project and filter Reality, then the Story, the script and the characters themselves change along with it.

A Sleight of Mind

The denial of Matter is what I call a sleight of mind. It is rooted in the very split-vision nature and programming of Mind which, in order to know, abstracts and divides subject from object, disconnecting the knower from that which it would know. Its methodology of knowing operates through a vicarious, intermediate knowledge-by-acquisition—by instinctively withdrawing from its subject matter, objectifying it in order to seize, grasp, comprehend and control it—rather than through a direct knowledge-by-identity which expands self to *in*corporate and *become* that which it would know. This vicarious way of knowing and being, then, intrinsic to Mind and mental consciousness, auto-imposes a fundamental ignorance at the outset, slipping in a framework of division over its subject matter of which Mind itself remains unmindful: A mental blindspot inherent in all Mind-based consciousness that prejudices simply by virtue of its *way* of seeing, running Reality through a mental ego whose mentalized Midas touch overlays division on all that it sees and experiences, capable only of conceptualizing Unity and Wholeness but not of experiencing them.

This inherent limitation, however, does not preclude or deny the remarkable ascending gradations of Mind which themselves scale to more illumined, rarified and intuitive planes of insight and experience. Nevertheless, these ascents, visionary and vertiginous as they are, still have their threshold, their luminous lid, still ranging *within* the realm of Mind, the mental fishbowl; still perceiving through its eye, its I, albeit more and more clairvoyantly; still bearing the vestiges of ego and its residual overlays, no matter how brilliant or fine the gilding.

Mentality, then,—the ego-personality of Mind common to all Mind-based religious and philosophical traditions, even those which claim to be beyond Mind—can only formulate and express Reality, however convincingly, through its mental filter, lens and language. It also shares an allergic reaction to light and exposure common to all ego-personalities, whatever the form, instinctively covering up its flaws, employing the ego's self-deceptive shadow-skills to conceal its presence, complicity, fallibility. If one, then, is to heal this schism so deeply-engrained in our species, if we are to reaffirm the reality and secret meaning of Matter and of ourselves, some core common sense in us suggests that we must find another way of knowing and being unmanipulated by ego: A *supramental*[4] way which does not merely transcend Mind, escaping terrestrial re-

---

4. Sri Aurobindo first introduced the term "supramental" and the concept of Supermind in the early Twentieth Century. This *Supramental* principle does not imply a Nietzschean model of Mind aggrandized and raised to its own highest power, but rather a radically new stage of consciousness beyond Mind.

ality, but transforms it in the light of a more holistic vision and power of being.

ξ

This sleight of mind infects not only our religious and theistic traditions but our atheistic world-views as well. For while atheism counters the tendency toward religious obscurantism with a healthy scientific or humanistic skepticism, it falls into the opposite trap, the opposite dogma: The denial of Spirit, categorically denying the existence of what we call "God."

This denial of Spirit is the mirror-image reversal of the denial of Matter, reflecting the same mental blindspot which unknowingly contradicts its own premise. For by virtue of posing an absolute declaration that God does not exist, it assumes the very form of absolute knowledge and omniscience it denies. A true skepticism, which is the legitimate credo of atheism, must then turn its doubt back upon itself as well, applying equal cynicism, humility and uncertainty. The most, then, that it can state is that it simply *does not know*, acknowledging a more honest agnosticism which has not yet experienced or found means to measure and certify another level of reality, intention or direction behind or within this phenomenal universe. But it cannot arbitrarily deny this possibility, no more than religion or asceticism can deny the possibility and potential of Matter.

Taking into account, then, these limitations and blindspots inherent in Mind as an instrument of knowledge—the sleight-of-mind tendencies which in one extreme lead to the denial of Matter, in the other, the denial of Spirit—is there a more affirmative and inclusive vision, a more imaginative version that, at least conceptually or theoretically, heals and reintegrates the schism and subsequent schism-making? Is there a more commonsensible yet comprehensive response to the How, Why and Wherefore of this

20

experience we call Reality, which speaks simply and sensibly to our hearts, sparking hope and a secret smile? Or are we condemned to a scenario which only promises escape but not fulfillment, foretold by a Mind enamored with the erudite and arcane, equating Wisdom with cleverness and complexity, silencing the laughter of the child in the austere and sterile summits of the monastery?

Involution-Evolution

Only that which is already *in*-volved can *e*-volve. A child, a flower, a universe, is born, not made, carrying within its core its own seed-self, its own unique genetic code of consciousness, its own self-rhythm of unfolding and becoming.

The concept of a Great Void, then, from which all inexplicably arose, need not imply the absolute absence of Being, only the absence of *manifest* Being. For despite the mystique of such a Creative Void, *some*thing does not come forth from *no*thing. In which case, what we call Creation is not in fact so much *a* creation—a Genesis mystically conjured, whimsically chanced or spontaneously combusted from some absolute Nothingness—but a progressive manifestation of That which Is and, awkwardly described in present linear language, always has been.

Working from this evolutionary premise, this universe, then, did not arbitrarily arise or arrive, but unfolded from some Self-Existence preceding yet paradoxically present within it. This unfolding or evolving implies a complementary process of *in*folding, *in*volving, whereby Self-Conscious-Being conceals Itself from Itself in a hide-and-seek phenomenon of Consciousness inspired, this work suggests, simply to explore and experience the endless mystery, joy and wonder of Self-discovery. In other words, for the sheer child-lit delight of Being.

Playing out this radical proposition, let us pursue the possibilities and methodologies of such an *in*volutionary-*e*volutionary phenomenon, cognizant that we are venturing into visionary territory that exceeds our present vocabulary, where existing mental language can only hint at, glimpse or approximate in allegory or image; and, in this light, where the intent, then, is not to *prove* but rather to *make more sense of*, attempting to bridge rather than deny missing links, to suggest rather than presume to define.

Involution-evolution, I believe, provides a more comprehensive metaphor and vision for cosmo-genesis. It also mirrors the inner and outer movements, ascending and descending spiral threads of the DNA molecule, reflecting in macro-scale that fractal seed/symbol of Consciousness coded in the universe's embryonic core. In this scenario, then, an eternal and ever-present Self *in*volves Itself and Its infinite Consciousness into an ultimately (and paradoxically) finite point, spiraling inward like the nautilus, like the galaxy or the whirling petals of a flower time-lapsed in reverse. In which case, the point where this Self is fully *in*volved—where Consciousness through an act of its own will *in*folds into Self-concealed *un*consciousness (a state which Sri Aurobindo called "Inconscience")—becomes the genetic beginning point for evolution.

This universe, then, comes into being or manifests from this seed of Self, imaged by earlier visionaries as a Cosmic Egg. This seed—this infinitely dense grain of Matter, inert and insensible—nevertheless (mind- and light-bendingly) "contains" infinity and eternity: contains all-sense, all consciousness, all possibilities of knowing and being, spanning from the experience of *not* knowing, *not* feeling (which, in terms of integral self-knowledge are still ways of knowing and being, still states, albeit negative, of consciousness) to limitlessly-luminous post-mental stages of consciousness in forms sufficiently conscious and resilient, sufficiently *egoless*, to bear an endless delight of Being whose intensity would shatter present nervous systems, minds and bodies.

Transcribing this in more scientific imagery, involution is the process of Conscious Being creating an ultimate black hole whose gravity pulls all consciousness, all light, all being into a field of unbeing. Evolution then represents the return journey that must somehow carry within it the evolutionary will, the Fire to Be,[5] capable of carrying it past the event horizon of this existential black hole, upstream through the extraordinary gravitational undertow and centripetal momentum to *un-be*. In which case, this involved negative state of Being and experience, which our traditions have described as some original Void, is in fact not the origin of Being but the threshold, portal and womb of Becoming—a uniquely creative mathematical dynamic where zero emerges from one before one can emerge through zero.

Such an evolutionary perspective would resolve the enigma of missing links: Of how Life and Mind inexplicably emerged from insentient and unconscious Matter, of how Matter Herself sprang forth from apparent nothingness, acknowledging that the principles of Life and Mind, the potentials of vital and mental Consciousness, were already there to begin with, *involved* in Matter, just as Matter was already there in the potential of Being. It would also reconcile the disconnections and respective denials of Matter and Spirit, applying the more egalitarian language of Consciousness— of a continuum of Consciousness that progressively manifests Itself in more and more conscious forms—rather than the charged and polarized either-or terminologies of spiritual and material which imply somehow that spirituality is a discrete or elite domain: is *what* we do rather than the consciousness in which we do it.

---

5. This Fire-to-Be, the irrepressible, creative Divine Will and Intention secret in Evolution, is personified in India's Vedas as *Agni*, described as "the one who goes in front" as well as "the sacrificial fire" that mediates between the gods and humans, sparking the human flame of aspiration that consciously evokes the Divine in Matter.

At the same time, this perspective would address the issue of intention and direction, affirming that the universe and its emergent evolutionary process are in fact "motivated"; are the Self-expression of Being, willing (meaning both "to will" and "to accept") to go through Its own apparent opposite in order, by contrast, to fully discover and experience Itself: A Self whose essence *is* the delight of Being—that secret raison d'être overlooked by our more morbid, life-negating traditions in their rush to claim-stake Truth; dismissed as too childish, too simple, too sinful in their obsession with weightier, more complex, more grown-up answers.

It Takes One to Know One

If Reality, as this work proposes, is conscious, is *Self-Conscious-Being*, then It is not simply an impersonal or intention-less state of awareness but a meta-personal Presence: a Person (albeit some*One* unlimited by our anthropomorphic overlays, egocentric projections and prejudices). In which case, It is not simply an *It*; nor a gender-exclusive *He*; but an androgynous *S/He* as well as something altogether beyond our mind-bound conceptions and definitions: An inseparable creative Whole, unlimited by any of Its freely-chosen limitations and Self-assumed forms, that appears or presents Its Self according to the local observer-self's level of consciousness, sensory development and integration.

In other words, by experiencing Her Self *through* this endless multiplicity of forms, selves, organs of sense, levels and dimensions of being, S/He can experience unlimited self-diversity within an ever-present Self-unity, tasting, feeling, being the "stone-stillness" of stone, the "amorphism" of the amoeba, the "terrestriality" of earth, the "humanity" of the human, while at the same time, remaining forever Her Self, Whole, One: OneSelf bursting into a million-faceted selves in order to experience the boundlessness of Being, the limitlessness of love.

All *this*, then, from the page one is reading to the sub-atomic and interstellar galaxies light-spinning within and around it and us, are forms, fields and figures of Consciousness: Of Conscious Being (in which Consciousness is the very *substance* of Being) unfolding Itself in an unbroken stream that appears to us through the device of time-space in discrete intermediary phases and stages. Of Conscious Being engaged in a process of Self-knowing, a peek-a-boo play (in Sanskrit, called the Divine's *Lila*); becoming progressively more conscious of Itself through various forms, filters and instruments of expression, sensation and cognition; most consciously expressed and experienced at present through (though certainly not limited by) the stage we call *human* being: A stage of being whose very meaning and intent is of a transitional nature: A bridging species, incorporating and embodying the principles of Life and Mind, yet whose destiny and *dharma* is a struggle to exceed itself—to consciously outgrow the limitations of its intermediate form, outgrowing the obscurities inherent in Mind and the mental prism through which we presently split Reality into Mind's[6] visible spectrum.

And it is here, now, where we find our selves, both in this evolutionary chapter and in this evolutionary moment: A species pressing and pressed up against the upper limits of its own present threshold of Being; pressed and pressing against a lid of Mind: A principle of Mind that has been both our gift and our curse, our first means to self-awareness yet our barrier to future growth, reluc-

---

6. Archetypal roots for the generic term *Man* can be traced to the ancient Sanskrit word *manas* meaning "mind". According to Hindu cosmology, *Manu*, "the thinker" and law-giver, is recognized as the progenitor of men, of embodied *men*tal beings. In which case the ambiguous and biased reference to our species as Man actually implies beings whose consciousness is mind-centered and mind-dominated. The fact that we are witnessing the reassertion and re-expression of the feminine force and principle of Being can be seen as an evolutionary indicator that our species is poised to go beyond the exclusivity of Mind-based reality.

tant to let us pass, to surrender its authority and supremacy, to accede to a higher, more affirmative, integral and fulfilling way of knowing and being—to a way of knowing and being that we, as that first species capable of consciously participating and collaborating in its own onward evolution, are now challenged to uncover.

For as a species, we are in fact the recipient of all that aeonic evolution that has preceded us: the torch-bearer of that Consciousness which threads and spirals all the way back through a tenebrous tunnel to that first moment of becoming, that first Divine urge, that Fire-To-Be which emerged through its own cave of unbeing, secretly passing Itself on like a molecular torch through our cosmo-genetic DNA; emerging through the attrition of time too slow to measure, finally cracking through the rock, bursting forth in those first proto-cellular life-forms, the forerunners of Life awakened and ignited from its matrix, its material chrysalis, blindly struggling and striving forward, impelled by that irresistible inner Fire-To-Be, that spark forever coded and kindled in the very core and nature of Being....

....A Fire of Consciousness slowly gathering momentum as Its inner will evolves more and more consciousness-sensitive instruments and organs through which to express, sense and experience Itself; evolution accelerating in micro-bursts, speeding up into more measurable eras and ages as life-forms developed more organized and complex nervous systems and brain functions; time itself speeding up as Life reached sufficient consciousness-critical mass to receive and embody the principle of Mind with its potential for self-will, self-awareness, self-development; allowing for swifter "evolutionary downloads"—for a swifter evolutionary unfolding, operating in progressively-more-rapid cycles, frequencies, wavelengths and vibrations as that Consciousness locked within the form found more intelligible, responsive and flexible instruments through which to free and express Her Self....

....Self now beginning to more consciously determine the adaptation and mutation of Its form rather than the limitations of form dictating the movements and constraints of the indwelling Self; Consciousness moving now at the speed of centuries, decades, years, hours, flowing inexorably now toward That which moves at the friction-less speed of light, the speed of grace, the speed of Being in an eternal present.

It is *this* Consciousness, then, this Conscious Being, that both presses from within and without, pressing us forward from our past while simultaneously attracting us from our future, inviting and impelling us now to break through our mental web, to consciously and courageously collaborate in our own self-evolution: The ultimate act of activism. The ultimately heroic human choice of self-giving: of an all-fulfilling selflessness which delivers us from and to our Self; of an egolessness which truly and positively liberates us, recognizing that the unprecedented crises sweeping our planet and our species are the inevitable form-breaking forerunners of our own metamorphosis—the evolutionary labor pains and contractions of that next stage of Being, that next *way* of knowing and being seeking self-birth, in fact already beginning to emerge, already beginning to ripple through our landscape, sending tremors and shock-waves which continue to gather force, shaking our mental and cultural icons, our corporate and institutional grip on things.

And in this transitional period of flux and intense break*down*, this terrible *Shiva-Kali* dance of creative destruction which till now has inevitably preceded all cyclic break*throughs*, we must retrain our instincts as an evolutionary species not to fear, deny or resist the changes, but to learn the graceful art of *breathing*—of existentially *breathing through* the contractions, working collaboratively with rather than against them; breathing through the pain rather than resisting, tensing, seizing up and unwittingly intensifying it; learning to consciously release our selves; identifying with the child, with the birth-to-come, rather than clinging desperately to the skins we are sloughing off, the reassuringly-familiar gravity we are outgrowing, the fossil forms of who and where we have been; letting the weight, the fear, fall from us, joyfully letting the adult mask, the burden of holding on, drop; trusting, surrendering to a more trustworthy embrace and flow, a truer gravity, even if we cannot yet see where S/He takes us; welcoming the metamorphosis, letting go of the caterpillar, the clenched fist and the chrysalis in order to feel the wings of the evolutionary butterfly beginning to unfurl in the sun....

THREE

THE ACCELERATION AND MUTATION OF CONSCIOUSNESS

Evolutionary Stress and Estrus

In this converging terrestrial moment, I believe the extraordinary tensions, illnesses, aberrations and breakdowns we are experiencing at the psychological, social, ecological and cellular levels are the direct response of Matter, Life and Mind to the evolutionary stress preceding the manifestation of a new principle of Being. The symptoms and reactions to this stress can be seen in the emergence and proliferation of:

- Unprecedented pathologies, neuroses and psychoses; dysfunctional behavior patterns, addictions, multiple personality and hyper-activity disorders.
- Mutant and resistant strains of bacteria and viruses; hybrid cancers, AIDS and other Trojan horses tampering with our once-sacrosanct cellular programming, mad cows leaping across the once-impregnable fence separating the species, immune systems and nervous systems dis-integrating under the intense "vibrational bombardment" of a new evolutionary frequency.
- Genetic deformations (particularly in the more eco-sensitive "indicator" species) and their corresponding neuro-social deformations, humans warping under the pressure, succumbing to lethal radiation levels of fear, doubt and negativity, going ballistic in school and workplace

shootings, outletting in twisted or abusive extremes, venting in outrageous acts of terrorism and violence.

- A hyper-competitive and carcinogenic capitalism metastasizing, infecting our ecosystems and biosphere, the air we breathe, the water we drink, the thoughts we think; infecting our laboratories and scientific research as well with the distorting cross-motive of profit, leading to genetic patenting, claim-staking the secrets of the cell, turning bio-tech (cloning, "designer" genes and births, genetically-modified food and agricultural products) and pharmaceuticals into lucrative market-driven fields.

Through the lens of this Evolutionary Agenda, then, these diverse symptoms represent the reactions and stress-distortions of molecules, cells and minds to the accelerating pressure of Consciousness as it approaches critical mass. In physical terms, this response of existing forms to the breakthrough vibration of a new evolutionary cycle is one of resistance and agitation: "Resistance" defined here as the primal egoic survival reflex to protect and retain present structural form and identity; "agitation," as the amplified vibratory movement of elements in a given field to a catalytic vibration, energy or event despite the status-quo resistance of that form/ field.

At the atomic and molecular level, this agitation expresses itself as an increasing heat, friction and elemental frenzy,[1] resembling the consciousness-equivalent behavior of matter in a compression chamber or particle accelerator. At the psychological and neurophysiological level, the relentless bombardment of this new agitating frequency, intensified by the counter-reactive tendency to resist

---

1. The English term "frenzy" is the literal translation of the Latin *"oestrus"* (anglicized as "estrus"); hence, the reference to that period when female mammals are "in heat" as the estral cycle.

it, translates as anxiety, trepidation and hyper-nervousness, contributing, I believe, to a spectrum of tension-based "evolutionary pathologies" from schizophrenia to multiple sclerosis and other degenerative nervous system disorders. At the biological level, the churning chemistries activated by the impending breakthrough of a new principle of Being manifest in erratic and often volatile system-level behavior, paralleling the organic moodswings and imbalances associated with a body going through radical hormonal changes.

These analogies, though theoretical, nevertheless speak to us symbolically, providing perspective, helping us begin to make sense of, even anticipate, the contagion of mind-body disorders, aberrations and breakdowns as a natural consequence of the tensions accompanying the influx of unprecedented evolutionary energies into calcified evolutionary forms and thought-forms. As a phenomenon, this dis-ease response to the systemic stress inherent till now in the nature of evolutionary change peaks as one cycle nears its end, climaxing as the resonance of the new overtakes the stasis of the old.

In which case, if these evolutionary disorders are in fact simply the crude but essential dis-integrating processes through which old orders (status quo states of health and being) yield, transform and re-integrate into new ones, then the extraordinary malaise and distress we are witnessing on a planetary scale may well be the prologue of a great mutation: A mutation of Consciousness operating through a meta-version of $E = mc^2$, where "c" stands for "consciousness"— for the liberating breakthrough speed of consciousness.

A mutation of Consciousness where the accelerating terrestrial crises themselves become both the mirror of all that needs to change within us as well as the evolutionary biofeedback mechanism mercilessly bombarding the nucleus of our cells and selves; piercing our ego-spheres, our thick-skinned layers of obscurity and unconsciousness; ripping away the illusions, shouting "wake up! wake up! before it's too late!"; reminding us in unambiguous material terms that extinction, not stasis, is the alternative to transforming.

A mutation of Consciousness where everything, in fact, serves the outcome, the resolution, the evolutionary *Tao*: Where all opposition, resistance, denial and suppression only increase the pressure, the pain, the agitative intensity, hastening rather than shutting down our impending criticality in a mutational process, finally, from which nothing can escape; from which neither our once-sacrosanct spiritualities nor our hyper-technologies can provide immunity; from which we can no longer hide in our hermetically-sealed laboratories or our ascetically-sealed monasteries (which, in their renunciation of the world and their abstinence approach to problem-solving, rejected and retreated from Matter to avoid the now-unavoidable contagion of actually dealing with Her and the humblingly messy work of self-transformation).

Paralleling the manifestation of these fear-based stress-reactions and distortions are the creative counter-responses, the positive counter-signs, already visible, of our impending transformation, hinting at evolution's next orientation, intention and direction. These include:

- The emergent species-level focus on Consciousness and human potential, in particular, on body-consciousness and the re-integration of body-mind dualities, beginning the authentic healing process of our unreal yet de facto divide between Spirit and Matter.
- The convergent movement (despite the antipathy and repulsion of traditional dogmas) of spiritual and scientific disciplines, inquiries, discoveries and insights, pointing toward a collaborative rather than competitive relationship between science and spirituality, recognizing them as co-seekers, as inner and outer approaches to one Reality.

- The rapid evolution and proliferation of holistic psychologies, hands-on therapies and healing modalities (from transpersonal counseling to acupuncture to herbs), reconciling the millennial misperception which left the body devalued and disconnected; consciously rebuilding the bridge that arbitrarily cut it and its embedded cellular consciousness from the surrounding continuum of Being; unblocking the energetic flow and interrelationship with successive vital, emotional, mental and yet-to-manifest planes of existence.
- The complementary evolution of conflict resolution and other collaboration-focused healing modalities, recognizing at the process-level our mutuality and oneness; retraining and reorienting us from our more primitive, divisive and self-destructive win-lose patterns of competition and of defining success.
- The mainstreaming of Consciousness applied to body-processes; evoking and infusing more conscious presence in and into the body via an expanding cross-cultural menu including *hatha* yoga, martial arts, dance, breathing exercises, meditative focusing and tension-release skills, dietary changes (related not simply to weight-loss but to enhancing moods, states of being and well-being); and the incredible explosion of consciousness-activating sports from jogging to skate-boarding to wind-surfing, from rock-climbing to gymnastics, extreme skiing to sky diving, pushing the limits, the envelope, awakening, igniting, firing up those latent spark plugs of consciousness seeded in the cells.
- The translation and application of this body-consciousness at the macro-level with the "descent" of ecology and ecological perspectives; reaffirming the de facto oneness of life, of our planetary body and the inseparability of her ecosystems; beginning the terrestrial healing process, reintegrating

with Nature, recognizing Her as our own painfully-disenfranchised feminine Self; no longer relating to Her as product or possession but as the ever-widening, ever-inclusive Self-expression of the Divine.

Each of these adaptive responses, I believe, reflects a mosaic facet in an emerging paradigm shift, an unfolding mandala of Consciousness whose kaleidoscopic pattern of oneness becomes more discernible and convincing as our perception itself evolves to meet it. In other words, as our antennae of consciousness, our sensory and cognitive systems themselves continue to evolve, clarify and sensitize, growing more integrated as well as receptive, we progressively develop the capacity to tune in a more integrated, holistic Reality, comprehending once-isolated phenomena as embryonic parts of an emergent Whole.

If this is so, however, if the intent of this new evolutionary principle and its subsequent agitation of existing molecular, cellular and mental structures is actually the infusion of a more unified, holistic and harmonious vibration of Being, why do things seem to be falling apart in response to the frequency of its incoming signal? Why the extraordinary acceleration of breakdowns, frictions, discords and disconnections, overshadowing and apparently outpacing the fledgling creative movements toward transformation, contradicting our very notion and expectation of what oneness is and logically should manifest in its wake?

In other words, why do we instinctively respond to change (i.e., agitation), even positive change, with resistance, defaulting to a survival reflex programmed to preserve status quo patterns, forms, identities, states of consciousness? For this default reflex, it would seem, assures the very stagnation, calcification and death of the form to which it clings, placing us in conflict with the movement of Life itself, which is to grow, evolve and expand into ever-more-complex yet integrated systems. Which raises the question, why couldn't evolution have begun with a more "evolved" and enlightened survival program?—a more conscious default that welcomed rather than feared the influx of a larger Life and vibratory rhythm, instinctively expanding rather than contracting in the presence of new energies and intensities of being?

I believe it is part of our unfolding role now as a species—as a level of consciousness through which the Universe is finally able to look at Itself more consciously—to voice these questions. In fact, not only voice them but begin to resolve them, consciously transforming that primal egoic "denial reflex" to contract with a post-egoic reflex to open, replacing fear with conscious trust, rigidity with resilience, resistance with transparence.

To begin this attempt, however, I believe we must first explore why Evolution "chose" this apparently flawed and conflicted survival program in the first place rather than a more harmonious, pain-free version. For if we can discover the meaning and method to Her apparent madness, we can begin to work more collaboratively with it, with Her, developing core evolutionary strategies to release the resistance, harmonize the unconscious stress-response that seizes up when faced with a frequency of consciousness exceeding accustomed norms; learning to expand receptivity to meet the manifestation of a Oneness we so desperately seek yet de facto deny; healing in the process that unconscious root-pattern in us that effectively causes us to flee the very things that attract us, the very things we claim to seek and love, including love itself.

The Birth of Ego, Pain and the Denial-Reflex to Contract

Denial, as I understand it, is the primal system survival-response to shock. Shock is the experience of an event or stimuli whose intensity surpasses and overwhelms one's capacity to receive and contain it. The more intense and unprecedented the shock, the more the organism tends to shut down, closing in on itself. In the process of time, the memories of core shock and unhealed traumas sink below the surface of consciousness, embedding in cellular memories that continue to influence system behavior, particularly when outer events reawaken these traumatized cellular memories, triggering responses that reverberate to the original shock.

If, for example, one has survived a near-death experience such as a drowning or been blindsided by the betrayal of a trusted friend or partner, simply walking along a similar shoreline ten years later or encountering the intimacy threshold of a new relationship may still evoke instinctive recoil, recalling original traumas, raising residual fears that reasoning alone does not have the power to quell. For these fears, this thesis contends, can only be *materially* released by going back to clear them at the pre-rational level: at the cellular layer where the experiential imprint is still lodged, vibrating there like a molecule of pain engrained in our bodies, crystallizing that traumatic moment in a material memory that goes on pulsing long after the actual event has passed.

To resolve and release that embedded negative resonance, then, one must effectively work it out of the system; not simply numbing or muzzling it, but replacing it with a positive counterpart vibration of peace and trust.

Exploring the roots of this behavioral syndrome, then, is there some prototypal event at the origin of the pattern?—some original event that triggered a first shock, first trauma, which in turn engrained itself into some primogenetic memory? A memory buried like an elemental grain of pain in the very core unconscious coding of molecules and cells where it continues to reverberate, subconsciously generating unhappily ever after that second-nature reaction to contract when confronted with the new, unexpected and unknown, i.e., with that which presses us beyond the egoic boundaries of present experience, form and reality, even if that self-expansion holds the very key to heal us and make us whole? And if such an event exists, what is it in us that experiences it as shock, interprets it as pain and retains the memory, setting up a genetic post-traumatic stress syndrome that anticipates the pain and reflexively shrinks back from it again and again with each future encounter that recalls and reawakens the original trauma?

I believe this original traumatic event, still subliminally influencing human behavior and decisionmaking to this day through its resonant after-shocks, is the utterly unprecedented experience of Genesis itself. For what could possibly be more shocking than that ignition and subsequent rupture as Being breached into Becoming, bursting "outward" from Itself, pulverized into the evolutionary stardust in which Self-Conscious-Being would lose Itself to begin the awesome labor and heroic journey of Self-rediscovery?

In other words, that moment which effectively birthed not only a universe but a separate egoic sense of identity and its corresponding sensation of Self-loss and un-Oneness—when small self was first cut from All-Self, shattering the Infinite into the infinitesimally finite, fragmenting the Indivisible into an endless division of "me," "mine" and "other"—still remains imprinted in our bones, vibrating in our most material cellular and molecular memories. For even after billions of years layering over the event, nothing has been genetically lost or forgotten, even if we no longer remember it through present brain-mind transcriptions. All the original embryonic material from which this universe was born still exists, simply refashioned and transfigured through countless variations and incarnations. In which case, the nuclear core of each grain of being still recalls (i.e., resonates with) the original atom-splitting shock and trauma of its own egoic birth, in effect, replicating in microcosm, reliving in each micro-moment, the unimaginable fission present at the birth of the universe.

It is this nuclear resonance, then, Matter's method of "remembering" recorded in the magnetic memory of each molecule and cell, which carries forward the existential memory of this unprecedented first separation, disconnection, alienation and isolation from one's Self, Source and Oneness; generating, I believe, the subsequent imprint that associates all birth—i.e., all experiential entry into the new and unprecedented, whether at the level of form, feeling or ideas—with friction and pain; each future threshold-breaching, state-shifting birth triggering that original memory; awakening that pre-cognitive resonance which translates vibrationally as trepidation, neurologically as trauma, psychologically as the anguish of abandonment, rejection, expulsion and exclusion, setting up a fear-based survival bias which instinctively gravitates to what it has been, clings to what it has known, preferring the embrace and comfort of the past and familiar to the post-partum transition into the unknown.

Yet behind this unconscious gravitational reflex, I believe, is a profound reaching back for the God which was lost—the God whose Genesis now from the "other" side of the experience, from the egoic perception of the same event, felt like a banishment from the Garden, a punishment, condemning us to an evolutionary exodus that, seen through our "blind I," seemed to only take us farther from that One we once were. Ironically, then, it is this very instinct—this egoic reflex to reach back for that painfully missing Oneness—which, I believe, blocks the forward evolutionary process to consciously recover It; setting us in conflict with the evolutionary movement of expansion that would eventually heal, whole and fulfill us. For evolution, seen through the Divine side of the equation, is simply the progressive outgrowth, manifestation and re-embodiment of that Oneness seeded in each grain of genetic stardust.

With the birth of ego, then, came the birth of pain ("pain" defined here simply as the egoic experience and sensation of un-Oneness). If ego, however, is in fact the pain-maker, pain-retainer and pain-reminder, coding Matter as well as Life with a gravitational resistance to change, then we must redefine the origins of egoism in existential and physical terms and timelines rather than merely psychological and emotional ones; tracing it back to that gravitational reflex which keeps molecular as well as biological and ideological systems locked in their patterns, orbits, structures, thought-forms and behaviors, auto-resisting expansion as a threat to existing egoic identity, stability and continuity. In which case, the psychological meanings and behaviors that we have associated with egoism are, I believe, secondary rather than primary definitions, layered on long after ego, egoic sense and reality were "born." In fact, much of these secondary meanings may well be the ego defining itself, instinctively diverting attention away from the painful truth at its core and onto its more visible outer personas, character traits and presenting symptoms.

While such propositions remain highly theoretical, let us attempt to explore their evolutionary implications and relevance through an exercise of consciousness, testing them to the extent that one can figuratively reconstruct a scenario billions of years ago, based on evidence only available, it would seem, at the cellular level.

Imagine for a moment, then, that we are again in that interregnum between Time and Eternity, that precipitous threshold before Life emerged from Matter. Life is still silent, *involved*, untroubled in its material matrix despite the fiery forces of creation that rage on the surface; still buffered in its womb of unconsciousness where all is still indistinguishably one, undifferentiated, protoplasmic, still sharing an unbroken atomic identity with its cosmic Source. Then suddenly, a volcanic cataclysm cracks the subterranean crust and once-inert molecules synthesize and animate, breaching the molten surface, thrust forth through a lava vent, expelled from their preconscious Oneness, orphaned and adrift suddenly in what for us would be a terrifying sea of stimuli: A sea of fire and flux where simply to feel the full chaotic intensity of feeling for the first time would be unbearable; and consequently, where the first egoic reflex is to contract, deny, reach back for that fetal Oneness that was lost: for the security, safety, peace and poise of *un*being, the painlessness of *un*feeling, the dreamless and trouble-free sleep of *un*knowing; Life drawn back toward Matter, toward its previous pre-sentient state of equilibrium through this conflicted gravitational reflex whose other name, I believe, is Death.

Descending back into that ancestral memory, in effect, re-identifying with those first proto-cellular life-forms as our own first egoic *cellves*, I believe we touch, at least imaginally, the evolutionary origins, root-meaning and sense behind the behavioral pattern we have come to call "denial"—a patterned reflex in this primeval scenario long pre-dating its more sophisticated and convoluted psychological incarnations. For to shield Her micro-brood from the enormity of that first sentient experience of Reality lived through an ego, to protect those first fragile life-forms from the unbearable sense of their own fragmentation and estrangement in a hopelessly hostile world of *Other*-ness, Nature's initial self-defense mechanism was to armor them in a carapace of denial: a thick layer of unconsciousness, dulling their senses, confining their field-of-focus to the fractional time-space moment immediately in front of them, rousing their awareness only to the barest minimum of consciousness necessary to function.

In other words, to match that unimaginably radical and traumatic shock of consciousness when evolution state-shifted from stoic stone to sentient life, She had to design an evolutionary device to temper the intensity. By desensitizing those barrier-breaking *cellves*, then, buffering and dumbing down sensory capacity and interface, She effectively reduced system receptivity to an extremely narrow band, allowing only an infinitesimal trickle of that unbearable intensity to leak through the primitive proto-nervous systems wiring those first life-forms, demonstrating evolution's use of ignorance to serve a greater wisdom—to protect us from that which we are not yet ready to know, experience or assimilate.

Denial, then, is simply Nature's circuit-breaker: Her method of matching system capacity and containment to the voltage of the stimuli, the experiential "charge." Too much charge overwhelms the system, blowing a fuse if not breaking the container altogether; too little doesn't provide enough voltage to stimulate growth, motivate change, activate (i.e., agitate) evolutionary movement, leading to stasis and stagnation.

In which case, denial, despite its negative human connotations, is an essential evolutionary mechanism, moderating and mediating that fine-line relationship (unique to each individual form and level of consciousness) between stasis and growth; allowing enough shock to prod us forward, shutting us down when intensity exceeds containment; effectively intervening to compensate in the degree to which the consciousness within the form is not yet sufficiently developed to bear, incorporate and integrate the experiential charge. In other words, the mechanical, instinctual intervention of denial diminishes, becoming more subtle, subliminal, psychological, as the consciousness within the form awakens, unfolds and becomes more self-willed. The contemporary phrase "pushing the envelope," in this sense, implies a willed movement to press past existing limits of denial (whether physiological, mental or emotional), consciously expanding system capacity to "hold the charge," replacing conscious will for unconscious egoic mechanisms.

In fact, one way to describe the process of evolution itself is through this willed movement of consciousness pushing the evolutionary envelope, progressively outgrowing the mechanistic need for denial as it develops the conscious, post-egoic instruments and vessels eventually capable of receiving and containing the full experiential charge, intensity and delight of Being.

ξ

While such evolutionary theorizing may offer new ways of looking at our notions of egoism, pain and denial, they still do not address the earlier question: Why couldn't evolution have begun with a more enlightened survival program in the first place?—a more conscious default that welcomed rather than feared change and the influx of a larger Life, instinctively expanding rather than contracting in the presence of new energies and intensities of being? In other words, Why couldn't the Divine devise a more direct or transparent means to manifest, bypassing the need for this awkward intermediary of ego, its inevitable companion, pain, and the consequent egoic reflex to contract? Why not just cut straight to the bliss if that's the bottomline anyway rather than slogging through this elaborate and laborious evolutionary pretext?

If we may presume to take the Divine's "position" for a moment in an attempt to respond to these questions, it would seem that if one skipped straight to the goal without experiencing the journey or process to get there, we would limit the Divine to a static experience of Itself, a state of sameness for eternity, pre-empting the suspense, intrigue, spontaneity, joy and wonder of Self-discovery. For how to fully experience and discover the infinite potential, possibility and mystery of Self-Conscious-Being, unless one begins from its manifest absence?—that is, unless one hides, loses (or at least appears to lose) OneSelf? After all, this is not simply a linear who-dunnit but a holistic Who-Be-It. In which case, the Evolutionary Scriptwriter must create for the sake of the play a proxy character: i.e., an ego in which the Divine masks Itself from Itself through Its mesmerizing power of Maya[2] in order to begin that voyage of rediscovery. A voyage which, after all, is not only a journey through

---

2. "Maya" is defined here as the Divine's creative power of Self-concealment rather than merely as "Illusion".

fields of space and time but a re-emergence of Self through fields of Consciousness, planes of Being, space-time itself spun like a spidery thread from that Consciousness, woven into a universe in which to stage its play.

Hence, the indispensable evolutionary role, however painful to play when One is in it, of the ego. Yet if the Divine is truly all-powerful and under no compulsion other than its own freely-chosen will, then it can bear to "suffer" the part (at least temporarily) of its own opposite, negative and denier, playing out the ego as the Divine's foil and fall-guy: The no-one through which the All-One emerges, beginning the hide-and-seek journey from unconsciousness through an integral adventure of consciousness and Self-knowing; unfolding from joylessness and all the stages in between to discover the endless, ever-greater expanses of joy and delight S/He contains; opening like a bud from Her Self-limitation and unfreedom to discover the experience of One's limitlessness, freedom, infinity and eternity; expanding from utter isolation and self-shattering to recover and embrace the wholeness and love hidden in the heart of each and all.

If the evolutionary plotline, then, is this unfolding of an ultimate mystery, adventure and delight of Being, then evolution's choice to begin with such a dense and painfully primitive character, egoic script and survival program takes on a larger sense. For if the whole story is about finding out the Whole Story, then the opening scene and much of the First Act would naturally portray the initial stumblings of an egoic cast of characters who had no clue themselves as to who, what or where they were. Nevertheless, at some point, these characters eventually grope, feel and think their way out of their placental ignorance, gaining a first glimpse of self-awareness, beginning with that Promethean awakening the more conscious self-questioning process that would finally lead us to the threshold of evolution's Second Act...

...Which I believe is precisely where we are at present. For the very fact that we can begin to raise this subject matter into the light of conscious inquiry seems to suggest a change in scripts; hinting at our preparedness both as a species and level of consciousness to move beyond the mechanics of our previous characters; intimating our readiness to finally outgrow our former evolutionary roles—to apprentice the part of a post-egoic persona and personhood consciously capable of rewriting one's script; rescripting that default bias which instinctively shrank before the challenges of our onward births; replacing that knee-jerk No with an ever-expanding Yes.

For it is the contention of this Agenda, as future chapters shall explore and develop, that:

- This egoic fear-based survival program has outlived its evolutionary utility, degrading now into its own opposite, threatening the very extinction of the species and planet it once primitively protected and defended; and that consequently,

- we are in that unprecedented transitional role-shift as a species where old genetic scripts no longer work and we must improvise new ones, new lines and passages, portending the beginning of the next Act and evolutionary cycle.

FOUR

BRIDGING FROM EGOIC TO HOLISTIC EVOLUTION

The Egoic Era: Life's First Evolutionary Cycle

If, as this Agenda has premised, we are at the threshold and transitional prologue of a new evolutionary cycle, a Second Act, then it is critical to grasp the meaning of the First. Otherwise, we risk repeating the same script, recycling around the same egoic center despite surface variations that merely change masks, scenes or accents. I would describe the First Act, then, as the egoic era or phase of being: That is, the initial evolutionary cycle which witnessed the breach and fission of Being into Becoming, the subsequent "egoification" of Reality and the emergence of a sentient "egoic sense" accompanying Matter's radical state-shift to Life.

This egoic era, then, represents that stage which saw the physical as well as biological birth of the ego, beginning with this gravitational egoic imprint of "me" in pre-organic matter and its corresponding sentient transcription into a primitive egoic identity at the cellular level. For despite billions of years of egoic evolution and overlays, I believe we can trace back the lineage of our human egos to these primal egoic origins, seeing in our more sophisticated façades and forms of denial the same workings of our cellular predecessors programmed by an instinctive bio-mind to contract when confronted with the new and unknown; recognizing in our subconscious human default to retain and defend existing ideologies, beliefs and institutions, the even-more-ancient behavior of atomic or astrophysical systems and their gravitational impulse to hold to present form, orbit and structural identity. In other words, to keep things as they are.

While ego, then, provided evolution an essential beginning point of consciousness, a focal-point identity and embryonic "I" through which Self-Conscious-Being could begin to individualize from Life's protoplasmic stew, its purpose nevertheless was a temporal one: serving as a proxy for the true Self gestating within it, allowing evolutionary conditions and instruments of consciousness time to ripen—to reach sufficient maturation and momentum—in order to release the authentic Self-Conscious Identity from its egoic shell and spell. In which case, the whole process of egoic evolution fulfills itself at that point where it breaks through the outermost threshold of its own gravity, spiraling free into a new post-egoic cycle to deliver the child it unconsciously hid, harbored and sustained.

If this is so, if the whole purpose of egoic development, then, is to eventually outgrow the need for an intermediary ego and surrogate stage of Being, then it is critical for our species to begin the evolutionary exercise of consciously identifying our unconsciously-inherited egoic patterns, mechanisms and behaviors. For by exposing them to light, we can apply a conscious will to transform them, transforming ourselves in the process from egoic to trans- and post-egoic beings; effectively rediscovering and re-wholing our Oneness as we heal ourselves of ego. (The terms "heal" and "whole," after all, are derived from the same Old English root *hál*, etymologically equating health and well-being with being in a state of wholeness.)

In this context, there is a direct correlation between egoic states of consciousness and existential states of ill-health, un-wholeness and un-well-being. If we are undergoing a mutation of Consciousness, then, marked by the radical transition from an egoic to post-egoic process and principle of Being, then the accelerating evolutionary malaise, distress and dis-ease accompanying this mutation can be seen as

- the breakdown and replacement of ego as evolution's principal vessel and vehicle of consciousness; as well as
- the mutational stress generated by an entire egoic evolutionary cycle's gravitational resistance to that existential coup d'état.

In other words, the present relentless breakdown of fixed socioeconomic norms and psychological structures, paralleled by the unprecedented disruption and degradation of biological and natural systems, environments and resources, are not merely a turn of events in some historical cycle that will eventually return us to the security and complacency of some former egoic comfort zone, but, this Agenda suggests, an evolutionary indicator that the egoic eggshell itself is cracking: That the ego has reached a point exceeding its instrumental tolerance and capacity to serve as the primary vehicle of Consciousness in Her onward unfolding.

Eggshells, after all, are not only the protection to shield the unfinished life-forms within them but the barrier as well to the emergence of the future forms they contains, reminding us that anything carried to its extreme risks turning into its opposite: i.e., when that which protects us begins to over-protect us, refusing to let go, it risks smothering the very child it guards. In which case, to carry the ego forward under this accelerating breakthrough pressure of Consciousness is a suicidal proposition assuring us maximum trauma, like trying to contain the luminous and untamable rush of an evolutionary river in a dam of mud or fishbowl of mind. If Mind, then, represents the zenith—the leading-edge principle and product—of this egoic evolutionary cycle, then it is the mental ego, perceiving and processing Reality through its mind's "I," which becomes the glass ceiling and guardian of the egoic threshold, reflexively resisting the threat to its survival, supremacy and empire.

If we are to heal ourselves, then, as a species, mitigating the transitional pain of the breakthrough, the pain which, this Agenda contends, is directly proportionate to the degree of resistance (i.e., of clinging to past forms, temporal identities and egos that we mistake for core selves), then we must learn the evolutionary art of "letting go," of self-*giving*, Mind learning to collaborate in its own self-transcendence; willingly participating in a transfer of power to a consciousness and process of consciousness which Mind can never realize, appropriate or replicate through its own means, methods and mentality.

The end-stages of this egoic era, then, present us with a challenge unprecedented in evolutionary history: A co-creative experiment in which the instrument awakens sufficiently from its inertia to offer itself to its own transformation; in this case, Mind voluntarily surrendering its mental ego, acknowledging its limitations as an unfolding instrument of knowledge, and in that humbling, lending itself to its own mutation, learning the essential *trans*-mental art of silencing itself—of silencing rather than relying on thought if we are to "hear" and uncover a new way of knowing and being, if we are to clear and reprogram ourselves from our unconsciously-inherited egoic behaviors, biases and fear-based defaults.

In any case, to assure our cooperation, the evolutionary pain (which, this work suggests, is the unbearability of life lived through an ego) will continue to increase until we learn to let go.

Core Healing: Changing our Genetic Psychology

To enter our Second Act, then, effectively manifesting the promise and potential of a new evolutionary cycle, we must begin the formidable species-level task of healing ourselves of ego. Practically speaking, such an undertaking takes us far beyond the moral, religious or psychological techniques we have developed in recent centuries to reduce, muzzle or tame the more obvious and easily identifiable forms of egoism and egoistic behavior. In fact, much of these approaches and techniques, I believe, are themselves mixed with egoism, reflecting the blindspots and biases of the ego ministering to itself, deifying or demonizing itself, defining and diagnosing its pathologies according to its own view of things, prescribing remedies according to an ancient egoic formula of denial of which it remains unconscious and unaware.

Clearly, however, we cannot heal ego *by* ego. Yet we are still largely run by it. The question then becomes: How to find a more profound therapy *and* trustworthy therapist, shifting toward a more holistic, post-egoic way of being while we are still enmeshed in ego? In other words, to actually begin this more integral evolutionary healing, we must heal ourselves not only of our egoic "condition" but of our egoic physician. For egoism is both an impersonal and personal experience: That is, it represents both an interim stage of evolutionary existence as well as a personification of that stage through the emergence of a corresponding egoic consciousness and its successive character development, reaching its present completion with the mentalized self-awareness of the human ego.

If we are to invoke a truer therapy and therapist, healing ourselves of a condition and conditioning that spirals all the way back to that core ego-imprinted evolutionary wounding which has accompanied us since the origin, severance and emergence of Life itself, then we must be willing to dig back through the helix of Time to those very origins of ego and egoism. For that is where the core of our malady lies—that is where, mythically speaking, light lies locked in a seed of darkness: in a subconscious dungeon where the princess of all true fairy tales lies asleep and imprisoned in a trance of unconsciousness, locked in a gene whose molecular memory still holds the anguish of that primal severance of self from Self, that wrenching imprint of un-wholeness (and, hence, un-health) crystallized into our proto-cellular coding.

It is here, then, in the very heart of Matter where we must go, *healing* our past rather than merely burying it, if we would consciously release ourselves from the gravity which forever chains us to past patterns, perception and realities; if we would break through the egoic threshold of the previous evolutionary cycle to awaken the princess-consciousness asleep in Matter, reuniting her with her Beloved.

The real healing and re-wholing of the world and of ourselves, then, begins at the genetic beginnings of the Story, with the molecular and cellular: with this primal egoic memory imprinted in the genetic mind of Matter. For it was there where we first "remembered" our pain, where we first associated Genesis with the self-shattering experience and anguish of un-oneness, with the wrenching alienation from our own Source and Self that, through the egoic side of the mirror, felt like the ultimate abandonment and betrayal. And it was there as well where we first "learned" that initial vibratory reaction we have come to call "fear," learned to replicate that egoic trepidation into a repetitive fear-based gravitational reflex to close, shut down, pull back, spinning that fear-born molecular pattern into an evolutionary post-traumatic stress syndrome which billions of years later still programs our reactions and denials.

It is at the primogenetic level, then, that we begin our true healing as a species, working outward from that nuclear core if we would change the subsequent biological, psychological and institutional patterns on the surface. For it is at the core where we still hold the pain: the traumatized egoic transcription of Genesis as Self-loss and the accompanying existential sense of abandonment, rejection and betrayal, giving rise, I believe, to all our ensuing fears of intimacy and self-opening; triggering that bio-molecular reflex to contract which, this Agenda contends, has fostered all of our egoic evolutionary patterning, survival instincts and behaviors; producing a survival program which itself now threatens us with extinction; placing us in conflict with our own evolution; setting us on a collision course with our own future selves; programming us to contract in the very moment we need most to open.

For in effect, this archaic survival reflex, coded in denial, turns our backs now on the God we so desperately seek, defaulting us to reach back for a missing Oneness rather than forward to actually *become* It; blocking and contracting rather than expanding systems and selves to meet the accelerating influx of a radically new evolutionary power and integrality of consciousness, assuring us in that unconscious gesture the very disasters, hyper-tensions and unsustainable conditions we are presently witnessing as we enter this Third Millennium.

If we would truly resolve these life-threatening stresses and conflicts proliferating on the surface, then we must change our *genetic* psychology, rescripting the egoic coding in our genes.

ട

Such a self-mutative process, I believe, is like performing psychological surgery on ourselves at the cellular level, in effect, repairing the damaged "carrier" gene of consciousness by replacing its traumatized egoic memory and reflex-to-contract with a new memory and corresponding transformational reflex: A memory of the future which *materially* remembers the Divine, *materially* recalls our core Identity and Oneness—seeing and reinterpreting the same event, the same Reality, through the lens of a diviner I; correcting the distorted egoic impression that experienced Genesis as Self-loss by replacing it with the egoless experience of Genesis as Self-giving; and in that subtlest yet all-powerful perception-shift, gradually releasing the cumulative grief and pain of an entire evolutionary cycle; releasing evolution *at the cellular level* by incorporating this new reflex of self-giving; breathing through and releasing the egoic tightness, clenched fist and reflex to resist based on the fear of Self-loss; consciously, gracefully giving ourselves to that evolutionary movement of Self-giving, letting go rather than rigidly, fearfully, painfully holding on to one's egoic littleness and mortality.

For in that conscious self-giving, that true egoless reflex and cellular release, we in*corporate*—that is, "bring into the body"—the real meaning behind Genesis, teaching our cellves to love, to expand, to give of themselves; consciously incorporating Love—the Divine's spontaneous movement of Self-giving—at the cellular level; establishing a new center and basis for evolution; setting Her forth into a new spiral by freeing our genes from the unconsciously-inherited mechanism that would forever keep us locked in our past: that would forever keep us holding on, reaching back for what is missing rather than giving ourselves forward to receive and become it.

By splicing this new memory, this new translation of Genesis, then, into our core genetic script, we reprogram fear into trust, the unconscious reflex to close into a conscious will to open; turning the egoic longing for the past and familiar into a childlike thirst for the unknown and yet-to-be; replacing the default vibration of doubt with an unshakeable faith rooted in a core certitude: in a *material* re-cognition that the Divine alone is the sole Reality and immanent soul of that Reality and of our selves.

It is in the cells, then, that we humbly change the very course and nature of evolution, consciously reconnecting and retraining our cells to an experience that had previously been reserved for our souls, in effect, reincorporating the Divine in Matter.

For with this new memory grafted into our genetic psychology, we progressively retrain (as later chapters shall explore) our interpretation of and reaction to sensory experience; updating the egoic perception of things as disconnected, alien and hence threatening, with a more holistic perception of the same Reality; redefining at the molecular and biological level as well as the intellectual and philosophical level the concept of giving in post-egoic terms, no longer equating giving with losing but with becoming that One to whom we give ourselves, becoming that Love which we give; reversing with this transformed genetic "attitude" our gravitational orientation and attraction from past to future, expansively drawn forward to what we are yet to be as naturally as our present default-reflex shrinks and pulls us back to what we have been and known; breaking ourselves of this once-helpful, now mortally-harmful habit of resisting, recognizing that defensive reflex as the very source of our friction and pain: as not only intensifying but attracting that which we most fear.

Because the preceding passage employs the image of a simple transposition of memories, one should neither underestimate the difficulty and delicacy of such an evolutionary endeavor, nor the extraordinary perseverance, self-discipline and discrimination it demands. For this is not something that lends itself to quick-fix New Age formulas, weekend workshops or one-night stands. In fact the process of core healing is nothing less than swimming upstream against the formidable gravitational undercurrent of an entire previous evolutionary cycle and its billions of years of cellular conditioning. Such an attempt, then, far from the exotica of finger-snapping spiritual experiences, places us before the other end of the spectrum: Before everything that still resists within and around us; testing our sincerity, dedication and motivation; placing us precisely before the very things, thoughts and feelings which instinctively oppose—which assume before we even begin our work, our experiment, that it will fail, that *we* will fail.

This instinctive resistance expresses itself most powerfully in human form, I believe, through the poisonous influence of doubt: through a subconscious whisper that convinces us before we undertake anything of consequence, anything that represents real change, that we are doomed, day-dreaming, wasting our time, incapable of exceeding the orbit of our littleness and insignificance. It is this all-powerfully disempowering spell, then,—this residual molecular and cellular mentality which talks us out of our attempts before we even begin them, reminding us of our gravity, keeping us leashed, docile and *in our place*—that we must break if we would discover a truer voice and power within us. To awaken from it, however, rescuing the princess, we must penetrate the stealth technology of denial behind which doubt hides, persistently exposing its insidious agents of distrust, hesitation, misgiving that greet us at the threshold of each new breakthrough, infecting us through the thoughts of others as well as our own, weaving us in their fatal web of self-defeatism that would keep us locked in our devolutionary patterns, blindly defaulting us not simply to doubt but to a negative belief: A core existential bias which, despite our professed faiths and surface spiritualities, simply refuses to accept the *material* reality of the Divine.

...Which would explain why our thousands of years of wisdom traditions and religious realizations have been unable to actually transform us as a species, unable to truly heal us of our core contradictions. For while spiritual arguments and discourses at the mental level can *re*form our way of thinking, they do not, as our millennial history thus far records, have the power to integrally *trans*form our way of being. In fact, these religious mind-sets have actually reinforced the contradictions and schisms, unwittingly aiding the egoic pathology by voiding, dismissing or transcending the question of Matter and the body.

For by practicing a negative belief themselves, resolving the problem of existence by the denial of Matter, in effect, pointing us *away* from the body, religions have not only missed the heart of the matter, leaving our core cellular egoic program unseen, untouched and intact, but perpetuated our species-level schizophrenia through creeds replete with harsh, guilt-tripping Father figures obsessed with our sins or distant transcendentalists who have no patience for such mundane realities; continuing through their scripts and scriptures to deny for our bodies what they claim as true for our souls; turning evolution itself into the ultimate guilt trip; pointing us forever away from this materially-corrupted "here" toward some spiritual "elsewhere" when in fact the transformation and healing we so desperately seek does not lie on the summits but in the cells.

It is this negative belief, then, this core existential bias embedded in our molecular and cellular genetics, that we must "convert" if we would shift to a new evolutionary cycle.

Evolutionary Triage, Healing as both Goal *and* Process

To succeed, however, in such a core healing, transforming the genetic conditioning of an entire evolutionary cycle, we must survive the raging symptoms on the surface. In other words, we must develop a species-level strategy that approaches healing as both goal *and* process, recognizing our "either-or" default tendency as a critical part of the egoic pathology and systemic unconsciousness we must root out. While working, then, to cure the core of our un-Oneness, our egoic malaise, we must simultaneously begin to practice a form of "evolutionary triage" that addresses the accelerating symptoms and manifestations of it on the surface: the bio-physical, psychological, social and ecological crises which, if left untreated, could kill us and our terrestrial life-support systems before we had the time necessary to undergo an integral species-level transformation.

For to survive the breakdown of the egoic eggshell and the centuries, perhaps millennia, of metamorphic transition preceding the breakthrough of a radically new species, I believe we must find a sustainable *trans*-human way of being; forging our missing links forward through an interim species and series of species before we can hope to manifest a truly *meta*-human being operating from a consciousness no longer subject to present ego-bound laws of physics, biology and mind. In which case, we must work from both poles of being at the same time: from either *and* or, core *and* symptom, moving from within outward as well as from the surface inward, zigzagging and cross-stitching back and forth from the psychological to the cellular, from what we call spiritual to what we call material, in order to mend the hole and reweave the whole.

This emergent healing paradigm, progressively incorporating in process the holistic nature of that next evolutionary principle and state of well-being we are seeking to manifest, contemporizes India's earliest Vedic vision that "one finds the Truth by the Truth." In other words, one must apply even in the quest the very qualities of that which is sought. A perspective which highlights the inherent flaw in all our Machiavellian-based approaches to health, wealth, warfare and spiritual realizations.

There are in fact numerous contemporary therapies which support, model and manifest this unfolding premise. For example, complementary medicine is an evolutionary cross-breed that incorporates alternative healing modalities and remedies which address the whole person at the deeper, constitutional level *without excluding* the appropriate use of interim measures—of more conventional medical practices and techniques—to attend to more immediately-critical symptoms and secondary-level conditions.

In other words, while we seek for newer, more holistic methods of healing, delving for more profoundly-transformative processes and practices, we must take care not to prematurely discard *all* symptom-directed therapies simply because they represent more conventional approaches. For I believe this either-or, all-or-nothing mentality is itself a primary characteristic of ego and egoic problem-solving which, in this scenario, would swing us from one egoic extreme—from total dependence on symptom-directed therapies— to the other: to that egoic counter-tendency which, in the more enlightened name of new thought or new consciousness, would focus *only* on core causes, rejecting a priori interim therapies as compromising or corrupted, regardless of their real-time applicability, validity and relevance.

In fact, it is precisely this kind of egoic mirror-reversal that leads to overstated judgments, New Age arrogance, intolerance and blame which, in their extremes, can be just as narrow-minded, heartless or cruel as their conservative counterparts, puritanically blaming the patient for their illness as if it was simply "their choice," "their fault," rather than a complex condition resulting from an interweaving ecology of causes, intra-personal, inter-personal and planetary. For in fact, I believe we all play, in varying degrees, an unconscious part in the background disharmony and disease from which all of us suffer.

To oversimplify things, then, in sweeping statements such as "you did this to yourself" actually contributes to the ongoing pathology at both the individual and collective level, taking a truth—in this case, the truth that we all must accept responsibility for our lives—and reducing it to a rigid karmic or mathematical formula. For while it is true that we must retrain our instincts to accept responsibility for what is happening to us and our shared terrestrial reality rather than slip into excuse-making, passing the buck and blame, we must at the same time avoid falling into the opposite exaggeration of truth, blaming ourselves exclusively for everything that befalls us. For at each instant, we reflect the unconsciousness both unique to ourselves and *in context with* the background Unconsciousness we all still collectively inhabit and unwittingly support.

In which case, even as we attempt to move forward from older means, medicines or habit-patterns to more progressive ones, we must remain vigilant of that second-nature default tendency to over-compensate from *either* to *or*—to polarize from conservative to radical extremes, throwing out the baby, the living reality, with the bathwater: trading our obsession with symptoms for an obsession with causes, trading one blindness for a more luminous one, flipping from total reliance on established therapies or ideologies to discrediting them overnight in lieu of more innovative break-throughs, instinctively shunning former patterns at all costs.

For it is this "at-all-costs" attitude which in fact can cost us everything; constituting, I believe, the blind Faustian bargain we unconsciously make in these lurches forward; innocuously yet insidiously leading us to trade off being true for being right; egoically reinfecting ourselves in the very gesture intended to heal us. Which is why to truly heal ourselves as a species, we must simultaneously heal the "I" in us which undertakes the healing, including the physician as part of the pathology and process to be healed, finding the Truth *by* the Truth.

From this humbler perspective, then, of evolutionary triage, the political as well as spiritual point is to keep ourselves and our planet alive and viable long enough to actually transform, providing ourselves a time-bridge through our intensifying species-level metamorphosis and mutation of consciousness. For in this razor's-edge evolutionary transition, extinction is the one price we can't afford to pay to satisfy that egoic need in us to be right. What good is it, after all, to insist on using only the most "evolved" therapies according to some arbitrary rank on a holistic spectrum if the patient succumbs to the symptoms? What good is it to cling to our victorious capitalist policies, still flush from their apparent defeat of Soviet-style communism, if that success costs us the very biospheric integrity that sustains life on earth?

Applying evolutionary triage, then, as a species-level strategy, we tread a fine line, combining sensitivity and compassion with discretion and discernment, recognizing that by over-focusing on symptoms and the use of symptom-specific "weapons"—surgical, pharmaceutical or military—without simultaneously addressing underlying causes, we maximize the potential for collateral damage while blindly creating the chain-reaction conditions for those symptoms to multiply, escalate and intensify; recognizing as well that by focusing exclusively on causes without some complementary intervention to contain symptomatic hemorrhaging, we risk passively allowing the problem to metastasize, infecting vital organs, over-running entire systems before we have found a truer consciousness and power to actually transform ourselves.

In this more integral approach to healing, then, one matches solutions to problems rather than force-fitting problems to accommodate predetermined solutions; retraining ourselves as a species to see through our well-intentioned rhetoric to the contradictions, oversimplifications and egoic will-to-be-right behind it; revealing beneath the façades of truth an ego locked into its judgment and prepared to defend it regardless of the consequences: An ego, we are reminded, quick to pick up new knowledge and vocabulary for its own use, self-gratification and self-defense; preaching avant-garde concepts while still practicing atavistic interpretations of them, subtly distorting truths into catechisms, mistaking and claim-staking an interim point in the journey for the destination. The point of the healing, after all, is to relieve and resolve the suffering, not prove oneself right.

It is this ever-so-slight distortion, then, between the at-each-moment willingness to be true and the fixated will to be right that traps us within all our ideological extremes, subconsciously fixing and hardening us into positions before we even realize we are "in" them or how we got there; placing us behind the barricade to defend and uphold the rightness of this position, the righteousness of that cause, whatever it may be.

What exactly is this default mechanism, this mesmerism that locks us into positions, policies and patterns without our conscious consent?

A Psychology of Matter, A Physics of Mind

Ego and egoism, as theorized in earlier chapters, are not simply phenomena restricted to the personal or biological world. Their influence, conditioning, behavior-patterns and biases cross dimensional borders, operating in the material realm as well as the realm of thoughts and ideas. Developing this theory as it applies to Mind as well as Matter, individual thoughts and their constellating systems of thought (ideologies)—like all elemental systems, galactic or atomic—exert a morphogenetic gravity and glue of their own, effectively assuming egoic "personalities," each vying at their own level for mental supremacy. In other words, just as the nucleus holds its electrons or the sun its planets, evolving ideas seek out and attract adherents, minds and means of dissemination through which to expand and consolidate their domain and dominion as they strive and struggle toward their own absolutes.

In this sense, the ideological ego of thoughts and ideas possesses us just as jealously and zealously as we appear to possess the thoughts and thought-forms which express it; ideas, belief systems and their emotional counterparts claiming us as "theirs" just as possessively as we claim them as "ours." This egoic mentality (in effect, translating a generic gravitational field bias through the membrane of Mind) operates and behaves like other forms of gravity, mechanically pulling exclusively toward itself. Regardless, then, of how inspired or well-intentioned the original idea or its recipient, this exclusionary form of attraction tends to *de*volve, killing the living, *e*volving nature of Truth, exaggerating and elevating the relative truth pulsing in each ideative form to an absolute, freezing a single frame of the film as if it were the whole film.

It is this rush to judgment and definition, then,—to claim and codify unfolding truths into fixed laws—that turns truths into lies or, at best, compelling but partial symbols of themselves; locking the process of their unfolding (and us along with them) into a particular moment and form; crystallizing and enshrining them into our pantheon of religions large and small, spiritual or scientific, economic and political.

The application of this gravitational theory in the field of human thought and behavior blends psychology and physics into a hybrid field of evolutionary research, opening up the exploration of what could be called "egoic mechanics": the intersecting point where the laws and principles of physics resemble unconsciously-programmed cellular reflexes and human behavioral patterns, reflecting an elemental behavior common to all "ego-charged" particles within their respective micro or macro ego-fields, regardless of whether those systems are classified as inert or animate, conscious or mechanical.

In which case, if what we presently call gravity is the elemental transcription of egocentricity (and vice versa), if human behavior and elemental behavior share common properties, patterns and characteristics in the same way that light is both wave and particle, then freeing ourselves from ego and egoism is the psychological equivalent of defying gravity.

What are the implications and relevance of such a proposition? And could this help to explain the mechanism in us which clings to its cherished mindset, defaulting to a defensiveness which instinctively refuses to expand or question the fixed orbit of "our" ideas and realities? In other words, could this theory of egoic mechanics —this simultaneous exploration of a psychology of Matter and physics of Mind—help us develop another angle of perception, compassion and responsiveness with regard to some of our more recalcitrant or aberrant human behavioral patterns and cycles, potentially leading us as a species to a more effective liberation and healing of those denial-based patterns?

For example, how do we presently approach and explain the phenomenon which converts once-reasonable and well-intentioned individuals, institutions or inspirations into fanatically inexplicable, inextricable and irrational extremes, dogmas and cults?

What is it that turns some into zealots or bigots while sparing others, slipping from idealism to idolatry, from personal quest to inquest and conquest?

While such behavior can be attributed to a complex of factors (including education, poverty, abuse, parental/peer modeling, environmental/cultural conditioning, psychological stability, etc.), this Agenda suggests that these influences create the ground through which an underlying physio-mental gravity exerts itself. The effective power of its attraction or mesmerism, however, varies according to the mass of the idea and the integrity of the individual, "mass" in this context being defined as the authoritative "charge" and momentum which the particular idea or ideology has built up in terms of time and followers. In which case, older systems of thought sustained by masses of minds repeating those thoughts and beliefs exert the greatest weight.

To the extent, then, that the power of the idea or charisma of the ideologue—i.e., the gravitational pull of the particular -ism, -ology or its messenger—exceeds the inner strength, poise and integrity of the person, group or culture in its range, that idea or its intermediary effectively takes them into its orbit, converting them to its belief system like mentalized electrons. (This same principle operates through the parallel field of emotions, where feelings, like thoughts, gather mass and cohesion, attracting their champions and devotees through the pull of what we call desires, desire-patterns potentially devolving to addictions.)

This "takeover" phenomenon translates through a multitude of expressions and degrees of allegiance, spanning from relatively benign forms of passive acceptance to the more virulent "fatal attractions": the emotional bondage, attachment or addiction to tyrannical, often self-destructive feelings, desires and their subsequent dead-end patterns and relationships; the mental enslavement to chauvinistic ideologies and their crusading spin-offs hell-bent on *jihad*, not merely content to worship or practice their own creeds but determined to convert or eliminate all other beliefs, ideas or experiences which threaten their supremacy, labeling such alternatives as enemies or infidels. (Depersonalizing this phenomenon and the play of more fundamentalist forces of physics behind it, these "infidels" simply represent competing ideo-gravities or, in their more conscious forms, gravitational outlaws attempting to defy the prevailing ego-dominant pull.)

Gravity as Bias, Gravity as Grace

Reformulating this concept of gravitational bias, this Agenda suggests that present laws of gravity are de facto the physical expression of an elemental ego-centric behavior common to all systems generated through egoic evolution. In this scenario, then, the human impulse to seize the truth of an idea or inspiration is, from the other side of the equation, synonymous with the idea's egoic will-to-be-right: i.e., *to seize us*. For through that possession, thought-forms attain and strive to retain mental supremacy; gaining our ideological reverence, homage and allegiance which, in its extremes, leads its true believers from the left or right to eliminate all competitive thought-forms and points-of-view. (The analogous application of this theory in the field of business and economics, which as presently practiced could more accurately be termed "ego-nomics," will be developed in a later chapter.)

This mutual "conversion"—mind claiming thought, thought claiming mind—in effect deifies ideas, -isms and -ologies; lifting them from their real-time relativity and relevance to the sanctity of absolutes; building religions and gospels out of political, scientific or spiritual experiences; freeze-framing Truth in the attempt to grasp and capture Her, unconscious of the fact that in that very gesture we imprison ourselves, setting in motion a devolving cycle of human behaviors, patterns and reactions which gravitate toward death.

(Death in this context refers to the crystallization of what was once alive, relevant, real. It is Evolution's counter-movement, reversing evolutionary principles and directions back into themselves; collapsing them under their own weight; luring them through the call of some long-forgotten black-hole core; animate reverting back to inanimate; fertile thoughts, like forestlands, degrading to deserts through a dementia that falls back into physics—that defaults to a process of crystallizing, embalming and worshipping the icon of Truth rather than risk actually *living* Truth in each evolving moment. For it is in fact this willingness to *live the Truth at each evolving moment*, fronting the immense morphogenetic drag and entropy of our past, that marks our conscious collaboration as a species with Evolution and Her upstream flow; expanding us through the gravity of each successive stage, each chrysalis and eggshell, like a molting of skins in an ever-more-integrated, graceful and all-embracing process of self-unfolding; emerging through the formidable egoic undercurrent of what we have thought and been from atom to microbe to man to become that One and Oneness we are yet and forever to be.)

"To see a world in a grain of sand," the poet Blake noted, stripping aside our blinders. If it is true, as he completes the rhyme, that we "hold infinity in the palm of [our] hand," the point, it would seem, is to release it, releasing our grip, and in that letting go, becoming that which we unconsciously held all along; revealing and freeing the miraculous through the mundane.

If we allow ourselves, then, the poetic license to develop the implications of this metaphor of gravity as egocentricity, bridging the either/or-ness of once-disconnected physical and psychological dimensions, it is possible to reinterpret the cycles of human history through physics; seeing through the orbit of our macro-human patterns the imprints and reflections of an ego-centered evolutionary cycle that gave them birth; recognizing in the cyclic procession of civilizations and revolutions that so often fall back into variations of the regimes, orders and ideologies they displaced the tell-tale devolutionary effect of gravity; revealing once again behind the façade of our upgraded technologies the same puzzled primate face.

In fact, extending and extrapolating this metaphor back in evolutionary time-space, we can track this egocentricity from its human to pre-human origins; following it back through denser and denser forms of gravity as it downspirals along an unbroken existential thread that links us inseparably to our proto-cellular ancestors and their molecular antecedents; tracing our heritage all the way back to that unrecorded amphibious moment when molecules first synthesized and synapsed, emerging from matter to life. In which case, the only difference between what we call physical or genetic laws—despite the apparent absoluteness and inevitability we have attributed to them—and human-patterned mentalities/behaviors is degree of duration and accumulated mass.

If, then, as Sheldrake and others of our species have begun to suspect, all laws at their roots are simply habit-patterns of behavior or thought that have morphogenetically grooved and gravitated over unmeasured aeons into stone-carved commandments, then it is possible to eventually free ourselves (and the Universe along with and through us) from the fated plotline, script and outcome of those laws through a process of consciousness that effectively defies gravity from the inside out. In other words, working ourselves out from the grip of subtler, more psychological gravities before attempting to take on the deeper-grooved, morphogenetically-established patterns which keep material and cellular systems locked in their determinisms. For in principle, *it is the same gravity.*

This evolutionary perspective and approach to Reality, acknowledging our common bond with and inherited behavior from Matter, would not only help us explain the difficulty of changing personal or collective habit-patterns, but would evoke a more compassionate, understanding and, I believe, effective response to them; recognizing in more impersonal terms the attempt to change such patterns and addictions as the attempt to reverse gravity, the degree of difficulty corresponding to the mass of the pattern (i.e., the weight of time and followers, molecular, cellular or societal).

Transposing this interchangeable analogy, then, from physics to psychology, if egocentricity and gravity are simply different ways of describing the same phenomenon, then the process of healing ourselves of egoism not only frees us of our mental and emotional gravities, but eventually leads us to the radical possibility of transforming the deeper default tendencies (laws) genetically coded in the material worlds within and around us. In other words, to the extent that we humbly root out the egoic reflex in us which contracts, pulls back, closes in on itself, replacing that archaic default behavior at whatever level with a more conscious will to open, with an ego-free gesture of self-giving and for-giving, we carry the whole universe forward, forging the missing links of consciousness that eventually liberate Life and Matter themselves from their unconscious bio-cellular and material addictions and constrictions.

Seeing the world, then, not only *in* a grain of sand but *as* a grain of sand, a cellular grain of sand, we begin to see through the lens of a profounder physics, recognizing the surface clash of historical forces—of religion and science, spirituality and materialism, communism and capitalism (or their conflicted spin-offs, internecine versions and fratricidal subsets)—as the titanic collision of ideological egos and archetypal ideas, the lesser and greater gods of Mind, each vying for supremacy, acting out through their conflicting and competing gravities. And if we continue to increase the magnification of the lens, penetrating the mental threshold itself and its egoic force-field, I believe we will break through to a world of far more primitive, primordially-entrenched gravitational forces and forms, governed by obscurer pre-mental gods.

Yet even behind or within these, if we expand the focus and magnification of our inquiry until it finally exceeds the measure of Mind altogether, breaching that barrier which arbitrarily divides life forms from material systems, lies a core gravity and ground, this thesis suggests, where Consciousness and Matter fuse in a single grain of Being: A point where no mental microscope or telescope can take us. Where the language of the scientist merges into the symbols of the mystic, the more fluid rhythm and rhyme of poetry better suited to describe and evoke an inner sense that can never be captured in words, never proven through vicariously-verifiable formulas.

For it is at this point of utter density where the infinite lies locked in the shell of the finite: Where gravity winds tight to its ultimate turn, compressing Consciousness from fire to carbon to diamond, compressing Consciousness into Matter, sealing the spell-bound princess in her crystal cave.

Yet even that density of darkness cannot eclipse the diamond light of Being radiating within it, cannot freeze the Fire that burns in the heart of all, emanating through the prism of the princess's crystal-pure heart, revealing on the walls of the cave the phantom shapes and shadows of the midnight gods of Matter. For it is these first gods whose dense, unforgiving laws of physics jealously claim her in their gravity; entombing her in a gesture whose seeming-strength masks their utter fear, suspending her in a state of living death; crystallizing her in a teardrop of Matter where they lock away the pain of their own un-being, worshipping the very thing they are fleeing; repressing it, enshrining her in an untouchable sacrosanctity where they kneel in awe and reverence before that One and Oneness they can never be.

For behind the terrifying and intimidating masks of these faceless gods lies an ego desperately clinging to us, to her, in a clenched fist whose grip conceals in its very forcefulness, tightness and tension the fear of its own fallibility, mortality and nothingness. The fear to let go.

A fear which can only be healed by a greater force of gravity: a force of self-giving which joyfully knows it has nothing to lose; knows, in fact, that it can only grow in the giving, becoming in that all-triumphant, all-healing and transformative gesture, that which it lets go.

Love as the Healer, Love as the Bridge

If we can establish, then, the possibility that human, chemical and elemental behavior share a common matrix, valence and bond, I believe we can begin to not only *think* a new physics but *practice* it through a new life; developing positive momentum around a new form of gravity, a truer gravity whose truer name is Love; in effect bridging the once-sacrosanct barrier between Matter and Consciousness; healing the dimensional divides between the physical, cellular and psychological; and in that healing, transforming the deterministic and fatalistic nature of the egoic laws governing those respective fields and patterns, turning them into more consciously Self-willed forms of expression, Matter conforming to Consciousness rather than Consciousness conforming to Matter. In which case, we are not simply defying but reversing the bias of gravity, effectively breathing and re-inspiring life into previously-mechanistic objects, terms, processes and systems.

Exploring this principle of attraction, then, from the empiricism of the heart rather than head, the secret, it would seem, is not simply to break the magnetic bond of gravity altogether, leaving us, as so many of our contemplative traditions and their Matter-as-Illusion orientations have pointed us, adrift in a transcendent Void where nothing any longer can claim or control us. For that is only a half-way liberation which, if carried to its extreme, unglues both the world and us along with it; unconsciously defaulting us to a negative solution that, once again, merely neutralizes the problem of existence without transforming it; throwing the missing link out with the evolutionary bathwater; ironically trapping us in another self-limiting ideology, taking the very truth that liberates and crystallizing it into a prison.

If we would integrally heal ourselves as a species, then, we need to expand our notion of Love, researching and affirming its credentials and efficacy not only in the domains of the personal and psychological but in the material and biological sciences as well; redefining it in less rigid terms as that evolutionary Force of Self-giving which, by virtue of its egolessness, not only defies all other forms of gravity but is in fact the secret magnet at their core, concealed behind their ego-distorting masks and intermediaries.

There is, after all, only one Force of Being[1] manifesting It/Herself in an energetic continuum from unconscious through partially-conscious to fully-conscious expression; just as there is only One Being manifesting in endless forms and variations of Self-experience and Self-expression through that Force. And if we split the atom of Consciousness, then, through this Love which fuses rather than refuses, this is the energy and joy we will release, this is the Being we will discover and become. Or, from the other/inner side of the same experience, this is that Being who will become us, overtaking us from within by a gravity of Grace; freeing us from the fearsome grip of unconsciousness, from the absoluteness of present ego-bound laws governing physics and biology; transforming rather than simply destroying those temporal laws; gracefully turning them into progressively-more-free-willed processes which de-

---

1. In India, this manifesting Force is recognized as the feminine principle of Reality. Through our present split vision that divides observer from observed, She appears to us as "Nature", referred to in Sanskrit as *Prakriti*; but in Her fully conscious form as the Self-expression of Being, inseparable from that One She manifests, She is called *Shakti*.

scribe rather than determine, bound only by the Self-chosen law of Oneness…

…A law and dharma of Being which liberates even as it binds, freeing us from the mechanics of fear and its paradoxical capacity to attract the very death it most fears; liberating us through a force of unconditioned and unconditional Love and Self-giving capable of bridging all barriers and divisions, of identifying itself with all by the simple fact that *it is all*.

Our primary role, then, as a transitional species in this evolutionary moment is to consciously call in this Love, evoking, birthing, embodying it in the actual process of our lives, transcribing it through our most mundane actions, feelings and thoughts, our breathing in and breathing out. For through this humblest yet most powerful alchemy, we infuse the Divine in Matter; releasing Her along with us from an egoic cycle forever doomed like a dying star to fall back under its own weight; setting off in that release a positive contagion of consciousness that changes everything, carrying us through the inertial undertow of billions of years, through the calcified crust of billions of fears…

…Irresistibly drawing us through all of our resistances toward a secret joy resonating within each grain of Being, a secret Self hidden behind each egoic mask; spiraling us forth into an ever-wider world of wonder; transforming the universe from a clock-work mechanism wound by egocentric laws to a living field of Consciousness expressed through an ever-more-embracing and holistic gravity of Grace: A gravity of Light whose touch heals all shadows, healing the terrorist of his terror, the capitalist of his greed, the ideology of its exclusion, the cell of its instinct to contract.

FIVE

THE TURNING POINT
FORGING OUR MISSING LINKS FORWARD

This species-level evolutionary passage, consciously forging our missing links forward through a progressive capacity to love, a progressive capacity to outgrow our egoic gravities and the skins of our proxy selves, eventually leads us to a pivotal turning point in our nature as human beings. A point where we are no longer simply *Homo sapiens* but a next species: An emergent species unfolding through the bud of our transitional humanity, just as contemporary *H. sapiens* emerged through a series of predecessors, mutating through more recent epochs of terrestrial time from the more ape-like genus *Ardipithecus* and *Australopithecus* to that of the hominids; weaving and sub-mutating our way through our extant genus *Hominidae* and our various ancestral branches from *H. habilis* to *H. erectus* and their intermediaries, overtaking *neanderthalensis* until we reached our present human station.

Evolving a New Nomenclature for Human Evolution
To explore possible future scenarios for our species, this Agenda suggests a reevaluation and redefinition of our existing evolutionary nomenclature and classification as *Homo sapiens*. The term "homo" translates from the Latin as "man." As a genus in the mammalian order of primates, this terminology carries a certain intrinsic etymological sense, since, as this thesis footnoted in an earlier chapter, the gender-neutral term "man" itself derives from the San-

skrit term *"manas"* meaning "mind." In which case, the genus *Homo* does not simply mean "man," but denotes the emergence of mental or mind-based beings.

The evolutionary designation "homo," then, provides a more profound genus distinction than even its name-givers might have intended, distinguishing its evolving sub-species from the more instinct-guided, instinct-driven animal forms, orders and genii preceding it where the principle of Mind was still *involved* or subordinate to the Life principle and its more vitalistic and instinctual ways of knowing and being. However, the species baptized as *sapiens* is, I believe, a misnomer. For the term "sapiens," from the Latin, means "wise." And while one can understand the intent behind the adjective identifying modern humans as "wise" relative to our tree-swinging ancestors, it would be difficult, particularly based on present species-level conduct, decision-making and subsequent planetary predicaments, to imply that we are a wisdom-based upgrade.

While it is true, then, that we have developed in ever-more-rapid mutational bursts the mental capacity to seek out knowledge and accumulate information, effectively becoming information hunter-gatherers in the same way that previous drafts of our genus developed more subsistence-based hunter-gatherer skills, there is a qualitative distinction between wisdom and knowledge: Wisdom, in this context, implies the more integral art of knowing how to truly use and apply the knowledge gathered—something which our species has yet to demonstrate.

If we are not de facto Homo *sapiens*, "wise-minded beings," what then are we? I believe a more accurate appellation would be *Homo egoicus*. For evolution, as this Agenda contends, has reached in us the zenith of her emergence in and through ego and the egoic principle, consummating in the present state and mentality of our species the ultimate development and range of an egoic evolutionary cycle. In other words, the end-point of Consciousness in its unfolding through egoic forms of cognition, perception, experience and embodiment.

This premise and contention establishes us, then, as that turning-point species where the egoic eggshells of all that has gone before us—the successive crystallization and calcification of the previous principles and stages of Matter, Life and Mind—simultaneously reach their maximum rigidity, threshold and capacity to contain a next (borrowing from Sri Aurobindo's lexicon) *Supramental* principle seeded and pre-existing within them: A next principle not only uniquely distinct from its predecessors, as Matter, Life and Mind are distinct from one another, but of a radically different nature, order and magnitude of Being. For the Supramental is not simply a maxxed-out extension of Mind, but a principle in its own right beyond Mind as well as beyond the entire preceding cycle of egoic-based evolution itself.

The Supramental, then, is both a mutation at the principle level as well as the cyclic level, initiating the first principle of a whole new post-egoic order and evolutionary cycle: A whole new chapter in the universe's genetic script which finally brings the Script-Writer, previously hidden in the evolutionary wings, onto center stage, releasing in the process once-tragic characters trapped in the gravity of their roles and masks to play out their true forms, figures and facets in a play of conscious oneness and unending delight.

This Supramental principle awaiting us on the other side of the eggshell not only differs qualitatively and substantively from all the principles of egoic evolution preceding it, no longer manifesting through the placental membrane and overlay of ego, but also differs in the process and method of its emergence. For it does not simply happen by unconscious genetic mechanisms, catalyzed by circumstances or imposed by a *deus ex machina* who presses Nature forward through the force of some pre-programmed fate, but rather interactively and consensually through the progressively-awakened will and intervention of the evolute itself.

In other words, as Consciousness emerged from the egoic co-coon of unconsciousness in evolution's first cycle through Matter, Life and Mind, molecules didn't choose to become microbes, no more than algae chose to become amoebas or monkeys chose to mutate to men. In order for this next Supramental principle of Being, however, to truly emerge and evolve, this Agenda suggests that the process of its unfolding necessitates a collaborative relationship and co-creative partnership with its prospective candidate; launching a new, far riskier evolutionary experiment and initiation of consciousness in which the outcome is no longer rigidly pre-`determined (i.e., mechanistically coded from within or imposed from without) but rather contingent on the free-willed consent and participation of the creature, in this case, us, willingly lending ourselves to our own transformation; willfully evoking, inviting and calling in that next principle; exerting a conscious intentionality absent in all previous evolutionary mutation processes leading up to this one; presenting us as a species with both a remarkable and terrifying choice and possibility.

In this context, we play a unique evolutionary role, bear a unique species-level responsibility, not merely acceding passively or reluctantly to our evolutionary/genetic destiny but consciously participating in redrafting its script; in effect, invoking and activating the true script-writer within us formerly obscured under sedimentary layers of unconsciousness and ego; and in that invocation, that first truly conscious *evolutionary choice*, willingly expanding our way out of the eggshell rather than succumbing to a dying egoic gravity desperately trying to still keep it together, desperately clinging to its increasingly-illusory hold on things and us.

That part of our humanity, then, which still primarily identifies itself with *H. egoicus* and the petrified past that is breaking up and breaking down, around and within us, will follow its gravity, drawn by its fear (which, as we have seen, blindly attracts the very thing it most fears); unconsciously directing all of its energy to plugging the dikes, patching things up; frantically yet futilely putting bandaids over the accelerating cracks, fissures and fault-lines generated by an evolutionary earthquake from within: An eggshell-shattering earthquake preceding the emergence of an entirely new principle, consciousness and person from its previous interim forms.

On the other hand, a growing portion of our humanity has begun to switch allegiance from past to future, from what is dying to what is being born; re-identifying itself with the birth-to-come rather than the labor pains of the transition; learning to cooperatively breathe through the pain and contractions; consciously lending itself in progressive degrees of collaboration to the emerging principle and process; rebuilding a trust between present and future selves; tentatively or gratefully letting go of the placental ignorance which once shielded but now would suffocate us, over-protecting us from our onward becoming.

This experimental humanity, then, switching allegiances and gravities from past to future, is our truly transitional sub-species— an interim race no longer predominantly *Homo egoicus*, Ego Man (epitomized by the "Me" Generation of the 1980s), but not yet post-*egoicus*; in other words, still vulnerable to the powerfully-residual influence, ignorance and undertow of egoic habit-patterns and perceptions we are groping to outgrow: A trans-species no longer comfortable in its own skin, struggling, despite the counter-pull of its vestigial evolutionary tail, to metamorphose to another species. A pivotal sub-species and apprentice stage of consciousness where we unlearn archaic, ego-driven instincts and relearn more present-centered responses; replacing unconsciously-inherited egoic reflexes with more consciously-transparent wills; welcoming rather than panicking and slamming the door on our evolutionary future.

ε

It is this trans-humanity which bears the crucial role and responsibility of keeping us, our planet and its life-support systems alive and viable long enough to survive the intense transition and dislocation of our metamorphosis; learning to protect its own future child, transferring maternal instincts from what has been to what is yet to be; adopting and practicing an increasingly-critical evolutionary triage to sustain us through the accelerating meltdowns and breakdowns preceding our core breakthrough; not only setting forth new priorities and directions to turn the earth-ship from the gravity of its present geo-cidal course but following through with the determination to apply those priorities, withstanding the formidable gravitational vortex of resistance that would reclaim us in old egoic patterns, addictions, mentalities and behaviors.

What, then, shall we call ourselves, this in-between humanity charged with a responsibility far exceeding its present consciousness and capacity?—this trans-humanity which I believe is the primary audience for this Agenda?

At this point, it is difficult to identify ourselves by what we are, since, for the most part, that is a story still to be told. Perhaps, however, that is the clue to our name. For if we are not yet a next species, certainly not a next genus, but we are also no longer in the fixed line of *H. egoicus*; in fact, if we are that branching point in the tree of human evolution which, at the egoic cross-roads, takes the path as yet untraveled, effectively forging the path as it goes, why not humbly call ourselves *Homo transitionalis*?—the first species to willingly branch, pioneering its own mutation of consciousness.

If we allow ourselves, then, the liberty to develop this scenario, extrapolating forward to peer into our own possible future, what is that next species *transitionalis* is branching toward? For surely there are steps, gradations and links of consciousness that span forward between where we presently are as transitional beings and that radically new post-egoic being capable of embodying a supramental principle in material form. And, just as surely accompanying these unfolding gradations, there will be extraordinary changes along the way, not only in the way we presently think, but in our neuro-sensory, hormonal, cognitive, volitional and corporeal functions: i.e., consciousness changes which eventually effectuate corresponding organic changes, transforming existing organs, systems and methods of nutrition, digestion, metabolism, breathing, etc. as we evolve more direct, conscious and graceful means to experience, communicate, derive energy and sustenance, maintain health, cellular renewal and regeneration.

One of the most common errors and egoic throw-back reflexes, I believe, for those of us in this fluid and as-yet-undefined evolutionary nether zone, disoriented and without a sense of true context or place, is to think we are farther ahead then we actually are. Or, as a variant of this misperception, to gloss over essential stepping-stone stages, skipping them in the ego's impatience to get to the destination without working through the process to actually get us there, blinded by its inherent self-deluding tendency which oversimplifies truth; naïvely leading us to believe that we just need to snap our fingers, repeat a few mantras, click our heels together and *voilá*, we are *there*, leaping in one evolutionary bound from ego to Divine Self—the ultimate either-or.

Cognizant, then, of our humbler evolutionary context and the series of species-level gradations that lie before us, I believe it is more helpful to identify ourselves as kindergarteners at the precipice of a whole new process of consciousness rather than inflating, glorifying and crowning ourselves as some highly-evolved species on the verge of spiritual mastery, dominion and power. After all, our entire history of religious, spiritual and metaphysical experience, impressive as it may seem from our egocentric vantage point, spans a mere micro-second in reference to the larger waves of geological time, proto-cellular conditioning and obscurity that we are still working through. And while each of our subsequent mutations accelerates exponentially through the action of a progressively-more-liberated self-awakening and self-awareness, nevertheless, the evolutionary race we are running is a marathon, not a sprint, a relay, not a solo, with numerous species and sub-species ahead of us to whom we must pass the baton and torch of consciousness, in effect becoming them in that synaptic transfer.

That next species beyond *H. egoicus*, then, that we as a transitional sub-species are struggling to become, could perhaps be called *H. holisticus*. For while such a next species would be radically different in its aspiration and orientation of consciousness from *H. egoicus*, guided, I believe, by what Sri Aurobindo called a "Mind of Light"—a transparent mind whose reference point for Reality is rooted in a post-egoic perception of wholeness and integrality— nevertheless it would still bear the residual imprint of the genus *Hominidae* and the mental principle through which it emerged. In which case, even this tentatively-termed *H. holisticus* is still not synonymous with that meta-being beyond the egoic eggshell and imprint of Mind which caste-marks our genus as hominids. For that *supra*mentalized consciousness, embodied in a form no longer subject to the laws and gravities of egoic evolution, is not simply another species but another genus, order and principle of being altogether.

As a theoretical progression, then, *H. egoicus* leads to *H. transitionalis*, which in turn branches toward *H. holisticus*—that future noetic stage and species which completes and fulfills our present evolution as humans belonging to the genus *Homo*. In other words, our onward evolutionary thrust moves us from ego-entrenched mental beings to mind-based beings consciously strug-gling to emerge from the divisive principle of their own mentality; aspiring to recenter themselves at their evolutionary core; actively working to replace that egoic center with a truer, more holistic self that eventually manifests as *H. holisticus.*

But if this hypothetical *H. holisticus* represents the upper thresh-old of the genus *Hominidae*, still birthed through an egoic evolu-tionary process, what is the genus and self-principle that begins a whole new post-egoic evolutionary cycle and order of Being?—that reunites what we call Matter and Spirit into something wholly other than what Mind, even at its highest, can project or conceive? A "wholly other" which can only be known through being.

While clearly over my head, I would suggest, for the sake of this exercise, the designation *Psyche materialis.*

The Emergence of a Post-Human Being from the Egoic Eggshell

As we are venturing into virgin territory, without passport or cre-dentials to authorize us, I appeal to the reader's own innermost commonsense as a compass-point and tuning fork for what rings true as we pursue this passage. With this proviso, then, the rationale behind the proposed term *Psyche materialis* is as follows: Since we are not just seeking to identify another species under the present genus *Homo*, we need to create a new surname that distinguishes not only a new genus but a new principle of being. If this genus and principle is no longer a derivative of Mind and mind-based men; if it is no longer an evolute formed through the previous evolution-ary cycle's egoic means, methodologies and birth processes, then it deserves a radically new nomenclature.

By proposing the term *Psyche* in place of *Homo*, then, we evoke a classification of Being distinctly unique both in substance and consciousness from the previous principles of Matter, Life and

Mind: A psychic[1] identity which, as the first genus of a Supramental principle, is not only another order of Being and dimension of knowing in its own right, but which, at the same time, is capable of consciously influencing, informing and eventually intermediating the transformation of the three presently-manifest principles overshadowing its presence. (In fact, this Agenda suggests, it is the direct influence and response of this "psychic being" and its corresponding consciousness evoked through the aspiration of *Homo transitionalis* that manifests in the fulfilled human version of *H. holisticus*—that last species in our hominid line, no longer governed by an egoic mentality but a Mind of Light: A mind overtaken by the holistic and harmonic nature of a next principle of Being, transfigured by a core psyche whose transparent touch frees mind of its egoic overlay, bridging through the link-form of this liberated and illumined mind a taste of what is to come.)

Having suggested *Psyche*, then, as the first genus of a new *supramental* evolutionary order and progression of consciousness, the modifier *materialis* establishes that this next being and principle of being is not simply a transformation from the neck up—a subtle or etheric change that leads to some luminous but disembodied being, trance or transcendent state—but an integrally-transformed consciousness manifest in a *material* body: A body no longer disenfranchised from the Divine by virtue of the egoic obscurity embedded in its cellular coding and composition; no longer excluded and cut off from participating in the divinization process; in fact representing the true liberation and fulfillment of a divine life in a di-

---

1. The use of the term "psychic" here is not to be confused with the more common associations reducing it to "occult or paranormal phenomena", but rather draws its root-meaning from the Greek word *psyche*, which, as Sri Aurobindo employs it, represents both the emergent soul principle as well as its emergent Self: i.e., the true individual, noted here as the *psychic* being, who incarnates and evolves through successive evolutionary experiences.

vine body capable of expressing in both beauty of form and function the Presence which inhabits it.

For the true measure of God's omnipotence is not the need to flee or transcend a creation forever condemned to second-class status, abandoning Her for some static or ecstatic escape when the existential going gets tough. On the contrary, such behavior effectively exposes a God still subject to the conditions of his own making, revealing behind his intimidating and exalted cover-ups the ego's tell-tale cut-and-run reflex. Calling our own spiritual bluff, then, the true strength of God lies in the other direction, in a far humbler yet infinitely-powerful gesture of Self-giving: embracing and becoming Her, affirming rather than denying Her, He becoming S/He, grounding Love in Matter—in a material expression released from Her previous egoic gravities, laws and limitations, capable of transparently reflecting, experiencing and embodying the true nature of the Divine.

This, then, is the implication contained in the visionary reference to *Psyche materialis*, providing us a focal-point term to complete our evolutionary hypothesis and differentiate our transition from egoic to post-egoic evolution—from the successive species upgrades of ego-centered, mind-based mortals to a self-emergent psyche-centered, supramentalized being released from all previous egoic laws, principles and processes, eventually freeing us in some millennial future from even the final egoic law of Death itself. For this meta-being on the other side of the evolutionary threshold, on the other side of the Ego's gilded shell, is no longer subject to the authority of rules, however iron-clad, which still preside within the shell.

If we follow the process of Consciousness, then, from its present intermediate human stage through its onward trans-humanity in an unbroken progression to its true, open-ended conclusions, completing in the process the circuit between Matter and Spirit rather than arbitrarily restricting our spiritualities and spiritual development to inner realms and inner liberations, there is no reason to assume that an integral transformation at the cellular level is not possible. And if such a cellular transformation is indeed possible, methodically translating into a new body and bodily way of being, adapting present organic forms and functions to more conscious (i.e., ego-free) processes, why should such a transformation stop short of reversing the last of our ego-scripted laws?

In which case, the human-bound imperative we call "physical death" may in fact simply be the logical end-result of all egocentric-based forms and thought-forms, pulled back into themselves by the entropic gravity and emptiness at their core. If, however, we replace that core, reintegrating ourselves from the inside out around a truer center and Self, effectively shifting from ego-centric to psyche-centric evolution, then *all* the laws and rules of the game change, challenging even the morphogenetic sanctity of cellular degeneration and death; placing it in a humbler, more relative light; redefining Death, despite its intimidating stature, as a temporal, finite law whose power only extends in the realm of ego and ego-based evolution; in effect, subjecting Death to its own mortality. For if we step outside the boundaries, biases and gravities of ego, then, we step, at least theoretically, outside the grasp of friction, pain and death.

If we release ourselves, then, from our present fixed concepts supported by the mind's illusory certitudes, in effect, turning the gravity of our doubts back on themselves, why shouldn't the body have equal access to that immortality presently reserved for the soul? Hence, *Psyche materialis*—the first truly post-egoic species to manifest a radically new supramentalized principle of Being and Becoming, materially incarnating that consciousness in individual psychic form.

It is beyond the present scope of this Agenda to explore in depth this psychic principle or to flesh out the "character development" of its sentient representative form, the psychic being, and its distinctions from our native human being. Nevertheless its designation introduces a conceptual terminology that rounds out a more coherent evolutionary context and synoptic overview for this first-edition Agenda, seeding material for future inquiries.

While highly speculative, then, this exercise of consciousness remains pragmatically-focused. For by pressing our present conceptual horizons from human to post-human, we give ourselves permission to explore and develop more creative future scenarios, exercising in the process a freer will in the course of our unfolding and direction as a terrestrial species. I.e., by requestioning, reclarifying and updating present evolutionary terms and classifications, we not only begin to forge a more time-sensitive language—demystifying arcane or archaic concepts, differentiating and developing distinctions that tend to get lost, obscured or blurred together in our more ambiguous and over-generalized spiritual jargon—but we allow ourselves the liberty to devise interim concepts and terminologies that de facto help lever and leap-frog us forward.

In other words, we create, even if only in temporary draft-forms, conceptual targets to focus and draw us toward our future; stimulating and sparking new neural, cognitive and linguistic synapses as we network and build our bridge to a being and consciousness which, from its side, comes forth to meet, assist and accelerate us on our way toward true identity. For this mutational process from human to post human is clearly a two-way process of exchange and interchange as we move toward reunion and reintegration: A process which from "our" side appears as humanity's present self calling forth its as-yet-unmanifest potential self, inviting it to incarnate; from the post-human side of the same experience, however, this metamorphic exchange reverses point-of-view, revealing a pre-existing future self that not only responds to that call but in fact helps awaken, quicken, inspire and nurture it, kindling that call into a steady flame of aspiration, stirring seeds of future consciousness sown in present selves, drawing us through progressively-converging synchronicities toward our tryst with true Self-identity.

In this context and equation of consciousness, then, "we are not," as Teilhard de Chardin noted, "human beings having a spiritual experience. We are spiritual beings having a human experience." I would only qualify this insight by suggesting we are either/or-lessly both in a transposable egalitarian equation where all equals one. For the Divine, despite our present laws of physics, is that One who can be two (or infinitely more) at the same time and in the same space.

As our sensory and cognitive instruments, then, continue to evolve, ripen and sensitize, and as we in that process expand our capacity to love, I believe we simultaneously develop the means to experience and apprehend the presence of this psychic identity sheathed like a secret flower within our extant mental, emotional, vital and physical sub-selves; bringing it into the reality-threshold of our conscious awareness; in effect, consolidating its presence from intermittent, fluid and unstable glimpses or breakthroughs to a grounded state of being that one day will be as normal to us as our present mentality and human-beingness. For it is in fact this core common-denominator self and self-experience—the emergent sense and sensation of one's psychic being refracted through the human prism—which has expressed itself for millennia through the varieties of experience which mystics, seekers, poets and scientists have described as the voice or revelation of one's soul.

Returning, then, from post-human potentials to present-tense humanity and the crashing realities confronting *H. transitionalis*, how can we begin to implement an evolutionary triage, providing ourselves and our terrestrial body the urgent symptomatic relief from entrenched environmental, socio-economic and cultural patterns, policies and practices which could kill us before we ever reached *H. holisticus*? How can we reorient ourselves to a more sustainable trans-species survival strategy and the subsequent wisdom, resourcefulness and determination necessary to pass through the vortex of our life-death metamorphosis?

A New Perception and Application of "Survival of the Fittest"

As a species, we are clearly in an evolutionary race to win ourselves and our planet the survival time needed to make the necessary changes before things are irreparable, before personal and terrestrial immune systems are too fatigued and depleted to recuperate: A race ironically where the very urgency of the crises and problems becomes the means sufficiently threatening to motivate us finally to move, to act, to change—where the poison itself homeopathically triggers a deeper process in us to find the anti-venom, the Oneness, before it's too late. In other words, where the threat reaches our pain-tolerance threshold, cutting through our egoic resistances, rhetoric, habits, lethargies, apathies, fears and fatigues; provoking that deeper process, that deeper *person* in us, to find and *become* the cure. The fear of death, after all, still genetically trumps the fear of life, providing, this Agenda believes, the smelling salts to awaken us from our auto-pilot gravity before we crash and burn.

If the accelerating crises themselves (as demonstrated by the stasis-shattering events of September 11, 2001) are evolution's leveraging mechanism, lighting a fire under our tail sufficiently-painful to overcome the powerful counter-pull and potion of involution's gravitational spell, interactively ratcheting up the pain in proportion to the degree we resist, deny or return to our somnambulism (in effect, providing us with real-time bio-feedback between our state of consciousness and the state of the world), then the point of our painful species-level learning experience, it would seem, is to finally recognize that:

- the pain generated by our egoic resistance *not* to change, *not* to transform, is far more painful than the change itself; and consequently, motivated by this recognition,
- if we would minimize the trauma of the transition, we must turn our survival instincts from preserving past to preserving future, learning to willingly collaborate with change.

This reorientation and reversal of realities effectively shifts our concept and application of "survival of the fittest," providing us the commonsense rationale to devise a more conscious, adaptive and effective species-level survival strategy. For to continue unconsciously following our inherited ego-driven survival patterns and instincts, coded to preserve at all costs present egoic forms, mentalities and behaviors, paradoxically *insures* our death—insures the very breakdown of the form to which it so desperately clings, shattering it through its own unwillingness to widen, its own brittleness, rigidity and incapacity to progressively contain and incarnate that larger evolutionary Life pressing to be born.

If, then, we are operating on an atavistic survival program inherited through an evolutionary cycle centered in the survival of the ego; and if we are at the launching stage of a post-egoic evolutionary cycle, then that program needs to upgrade unless we want to go down with the ship, joining the growing list of species we have already unwittingly committed to extinction. In fact, not simply joining that list as just another name, but bearing the inglorious distinction as that species who, through its egoic ignorance, perversion and misuse of power, oversaw the devolution of a once-fertile earth into a desolate moon.

In which case, to avoid this pyrrhic accolade and epitaph, we must humbly but decisively move from *H. egoicus* to *transitionalis*, consciously redirecting ourselves with the one-pointed urgency of a woman in labor toward the birth-to-come; adapting and adopting in the process a corresponding new "survival instinct" to deliver the child; transferring focus and value from the perpetuation of past egoic forms, identities, methods of knowing and being to post-egoic goals and the holistic processes to realize them.

This redefined concept of survival of the fittest, then, moves us from one which at all costs valued selfishness and egoic self-interest—rewarding crude strength, aggression, cleverness, deception and domination—to one which expands the definition of self and self-interest to include *all*; realistically rather than idealistically re-identifying ourselves with the fate of the whole; pragmatically recognizing that personal survival is *in fact* inseparable from the survival of the whole. In which case, self*less*ness becomes the humble means to Self-*full*ness in a scenario that redefines "fittest" as the most adaptable, resilient, egoless and self-giving. In other words, as that which effectively presents both in physical and psychological terms the least friction, resistance and rigidity—i.e., the least *stuckness*—to the inexorable pressure of evolutionary growth; learning to gracefully and gratefully go with Her flow. For true strength and evolutionary heroism in this scenario lies in the giving, not the taking, in self-opening rather than a clenched fist.

The practice of egolessness, then, at this critical evolutionary juncture, is no longer just a question of ethics, ideals or do-goodism, but of personal and planetary survival, shifting the matter from morality to mortality.

The Responsibility of Power

As this chapter has attempted to establish, the movement from our present station in human consciousness to a post-egoic state of being is a progression through various gradations, stages and micro-bursts rather than one all-at-once evolutionary leap. For such a transition-less leap, I believe, would shatter present ego-forms, like trying to capture an ocean in a fishbowl. These successive mutations, then, in effect parallel and demarcate our evolving degrees of egolessness, accelerating in inverse proportion to ego. For the capacity to contain the influx and intensity of a new evolutionary principle and power of Being, overwriting the denial-response to the shock of such an inflow, increases relative to the progressive expansion and transparence (i.e., egolessness) of the vessel or *adhar* of consciousness that would embody and incarnate it.

The will, then, simply to know, to seek and access greater knowledge, does not in itself guarantee genuine progress toward our truer future and truer self. For if this will-to-know still remains at the service of ego and its will to vicariously have what it cannot be; if knowledge and the corresponding power that comes with it is used for the gratification and aggrandizement of the ego's range of powers and realizations, we are headed toward delusion and disaster.

In fact, the warning sirens for this darker scenario began sounding in the mid-Twentieth Century, mushrooming into the Cold War during that period which saw the rise of what Eisenhower called "the military-industrial complex": A volatile collusion, demonstrating the dangers of a dwarf consciousness dabbling with the energy and "profitability" of the atom before discovering the true force of love at our nuclear core. This axis of money and might, then, catalyzed the emergence and ascendance of an egoic mutant—an ego-consciousness which paradoxically shrank the more it inflated, greedily harnessing the emergent evolutionary insights and powers for its own petty purposes and visions; acquiring and subjugating them as the means to compensate for an inner poverty, emptiness and impotence that it remains prepared to deny and defend at all costs.

In the material domain, then, the ego's fatal attraction to power translated through the creation of a technology and "development" mindset spinning precipitously out of control, guided only by value-blind rules of competition, self-interest and greed. In the parallel inner realms of reality, the ego—enamored by the same attraction, compensating for the same core inadequacies that drive corporate control mechanisms—sublimated these grosser material-istic desires into "spiritual" desires, seeking to satisfy them through the mastery and acquisition of "occult technologies," *siddhis*[2] and their enhanced paranormal powers; effectively placing these subtler energetic arts, powers and prosperities in the hands of a self-cen-tered sorcerer's apprentice.

A progressive egolessness, sincerity and humility, then,—quali-ties, I believe, supported and nurtured by that psychic being in us to whom they are native—are essential pre-conditions to prepare us individually and as a species for the right use of power and will. In fact, this Agenda contends, our very survival through this evolu-tionary initiation and its fiery rite of passage depends on these adaptive qualities; predicated on the selfless understanding that what we call "our" will, "our" power, in fact belongs to a diviner, infinitely-wiser and more compassionate Self we have yet to be-come. In which case, we must replace the egoic reflex-to-possess with the will to be trustworthy intermediaries, stewards and trust-ees for this emergent Evolutionary Power; consciously initiated into its right use and the ways to receive it; willingly surrendering all egoic motivation, attraction and claim for that Power in the hum-bling recognition that what is all-creative in the hands of the Divine turns all-destructive in the grip of the ego.

---

2. The Sanskrit term "*siddhi*" refers to realizations, generally mastered by yogis and adepts, that we, in our present human reality, would call miracles. These powers and practices, found in all occult and shamanic traditions, but particularly developed in India, Tibet and China, would include such things as the ability to levitate, prolong life, hold one's breath or control one's autonomic and metabolic functions at will. It is the contention of this Agenda that such *siddhis*, rather than remaining sought-after realiza-tions for personal power (which, at the same time, risks the ego-vulner-abilities that accompany such pursuits and motivations), will become natu-ral consequences and grounded qualities of a next evolutionary principle and post-egoic way of being.

It is in fact this self-purification from ego which, I believe, is the real inner meaning behind all our spiritual and shamanic rites to clear, cleanse and purify prior to initiation. For the intent is to create a true attitude, state of transparence and receptivity, performing a sacrifice which does not simply default to the negative—in this case, declaring all power as evil, throwing the baby out with the bathwater—but rather sheds the distorting egoic overlay that would *own* that power. It is not, after all, power that is corruptive but ego: a key evolutionary distinction if we would fulfill our species-level destiny. For if we continue to run from power for fear of getting burned by it; if we allow our fear-based impulse to lead us, programming us to reject and deny power as a curse, proclaiming passivity as the cure for its misuse, we unwittingly play into the ego's hands, effectively relinquishing power to those who have no such hesitations to wield it.

Correcting this fear-conditioned reflex, then, accepting our evolutionary responsibility to learn the selfless art and authentically-heroic application of power—i.e., learning how to receive without laying claim to that which we receive—is critical to our transition from *Homo egoicus* to *holisticus*. For the confusion that would have us simply shun power as the solution to the problem—a confusion subliminally or categorically supported by our more passive ideologies and spiritualities—would not merely render us a more impotent and disempowered version of *egoicus*; but it would leave us that much more at the mercy and prey of power-abusers, in effect, appeasing and conceding to their appetites, shifting the balance of power that much more toward exploitation, assuring us the very tyranny, perversion and destructive reign of power we fear.

If, on the other hand, we would turn the scenario creative, truly resolving the matter, the secret, it would seem, lies in learning to receive and accept power without laying claim to it rather than egoically blocking or attempting to control it; turning power through that "letting go" from an egoic force of division and suppression to a Self-guided force of Oneness; transforming it through the practice of egolessness into a conscious power of Love. For only such a purified Power, surrendered back to the will, wisdom and compassion inherent within it, can protect us in this life-death evolutionary moment from our own ego-embedded blindness. It is not, after all, the caterpillar that controls or oversees its own metamorphosis.

Distinguishing Evolutionary Goals, Means, and Mutational Timeframes

As an evolutionary yard-stick, then, we can begin to measure the mutational movement of our evolving consciousness in terms of a progressive egolessness; affirming a new survival strategy which paradoxically recognizes that the more egoless we become, the more truly powerful we become. For in the process, we acquire the selfless wisdom, liberated will and efficacy in action capable of mitigating and eventually healing ourselves of the species-level pain and trauma of our transition; in effect, developing the capacity to "tolerate" the increasing intensity and inflow of a new evolutionary power of Being by consciously diminishing the egoic resistances which generate the frictional heat and pain.

It is in fact this critical relationship between the presence of ego and the presence of pain that keeps us honest, preventing us from endlessly defaulting into denial. For were it not for the *undeniable* experience of physical pain, I believe we would continue to follow our egoic path of least resistance to the end, simply designing more clever self-deceits and denial systems rather than face the uphill gravity and challenge of change. But the body has no such capacity for endless self-deception and denial. In fact, despite its apparent density, the physical body is our most transparent mirror, humbly reflecting through the bio-feedback of illness and anguish the lies and disharmonies we would go on burying and suppressing at the psychological and emotional levels.

For the body, then, the buck stops here, mirroring back to us in unmistakable personal or planetary terms what we would otherwise, if we had the option, hide from ourselves forever. In which case, this body-reality not only provides us a profounder motivation and unvarnished sense of urgency to consciously collaborate with evolutionary change; but also keeps this inquiry into our future from slipping into irrelevance. For without the reality-check of pain, without the physical body reminding us that the buck stops here, this Evolutionary Agenda itself could easily slip into just another plaything or mind-game for the ego—another self-indulgent intellectual exercise which eventually devolves into materially-irrelevant speculation. The purpose of this Agenda, however, is not to *think* a new life but to *live* one.

Prioritizing things, then, in pragmatic triage-fashion, creating an evolving, multi-layered Evolutionary Agenda for the coming millennia, is not an extra-curricula activity or optional speculative pursuit but a matter of survival: a required species-level course for our twenty-first century curriculum if we would hope to graduate rather than be sent back to repeat another billion-year semester all over again. In this light (or darkness, as the case may be), the initiative for such an Agenda is not something to be left exclusively to our pundits, PhDs or politicians. For in this unprecedented evolutionary venture into the uncharted territory of ourselves, faced as we are with drafting, improvising and revising the instruction manuals and guides as we de facto forge the path, we are all equally co-dependent, co-responsible. And if *we* do not do it *now*, who will and when?

In this context, then, the role and timeline of *H. transitionalis*— our branching trans-humanity—is both the briefest yet most critical in the metamorphic process. For if we do not find effective ways to correct our present course, implementing evolutionary policies and actions to stabilize our most life-threatened planetary systems; if we do not immediately address the most virulent terrestrial symptoms rather than Nero-fiddling our way through the coming years, re-electing status quo clones of mediocrity, in effect merely devising better secular or spiritual denial systems, we will never get to *H. holisticus*!

The evolutionary timeframe, then, for our trans-human shift, fulfilling the destiny and responsibility of *H. transitionalis*, is measured, I believe, in the intense life-span of decades. For only after we have stabilized critical immune and life-support systems, allowing our species and planet time to recuperate and heal, can we can release ourselves to undertake the larger, more rhythmic transition through *H. holisticus*—through a holistic humanity emerging from the residual undertow of ego into the more harmonious movements of a Mind of Light.

In which case, the movement and emergence of *holisticus* from *transitionalis* suggests a more graceful evolutionary process of unfolding: An unfolding no longer leveraged by the cruder, more imminently life-threatening blindnesses, behaviors and abuses inherited and fronted by *transitionalis*. The flowering, then, of *holisticus* portends a species-level breather—a more rhythmic way of breathing and birthing through the egoic tension and contractions from which we (hopefully) emerged. For it marks the successful passage through the volatility and mortal dangers presently confronting our terrestrial trans-humanity in its most vulnerable inter-morphic phase.

Such a progressive release of evolutionary tension accompanying our emergence into wider and wiser versions of ourselves, in effect, expands time-rhythms; releasing time-urgencies from the more symptom-directed triage of decades to the centuries that our profounder metamorphic changes may involve; allowing us to more consciously undertake subtler levels of healing and integration; addressing the deeper tissue of transformational change.

However, even the expanded breathing room and mutational timeframes of a holistically-centered humanity may still not be sufficient to incorporate the evolutionary changes that bridge us to a truly meta-being in a fully supramentalized body. For the integral shift from the egoic mentality and mortality of the genus *Hominidae*—from human beings in human bodies—to that of a self-emergent being (tentatively-termed *Psyche materialis*) with its radically new organic/cellular structure, functioning and body may still, in earth-terms, require millennia.

While keeping these core goals in mind, then, humbly stoking the evolutionary Fire at our innermost center of being, we must stay grounded, focused on the immediate terrestrial-level symptoms in front of us: The psychological, ecological, economic and political crises which, if we indulge in spiritual daydreaming, will metastasize out of control. What good is it, after all, to poeticize about meditating under the bodhi tree if there are no trees left?

This evolutionary approach to Reality—distinguishing shifts of consciousness in terms of graduated mutations and their corresponding physical changes rather than lumping the whole thing together in one generic spiritual leap to what we call "spiritually-realized beings"—provides, I believe, both a more informative map for change as well as a more dynamic model of consciousness than the map and model presented through classical spiritualities, scriptures and their respective terminologies. For such traditions still tend to present Reality in static either-or concepts: i.e., either we are in ignorance or we are fully-liberated/god-realized beings; either we are in ego or in the Divine. In addition, these spiritualities tend to communicate through terms without really defining or differentiating them, commonly referring to things like "mind," "God," "spirit" and "soul" interchangeably, leaving the seeker to assume meaning, to assume we are all on the same page, speaking the same language.

If Life, then, is a *living* rather than *arbitrary* process of unfolding, incrementally yet integrally moving forward in an unbroken cellular continuum, why should Consciousness not reflect that same continuum? unfolding in progressively-more-integral and dimensional degrees, punctuated by micro-bursts and quantum leaps at synaptic points of critical conscious mass? In which case, working from a dynamic evolutionary model for Consciousness and Self-realization rather than a static spiritual model, I believe we need to reevaluate traditional spiritual objectives and directions accordingly; appropriately revaluing them when necessary from static end-points and goals in themselves to evolutionary means for future growth. In other words, revising them from fixed destinations in the journey to transit stations, rest points and rites of passage.

Evolution's Grand Conspiracy: Delivering Delight of Being

Virtually all our religious and spiritual hierarchies, theistic or non-theistic, have ordained the realizations of peace and inner silence as primary goals, developing and codifying entire ideologies, disciplines and methodologies to attain these states. If, however, we are to avoid the egoic trap of crystallizing such essential inner realizations into dead-end goals and ideologies, mistaking interim goals for final ones, we must redefine their roles, evolutionizing our hierarchical arrangements from fixed to open-ended; reminding ourselves that if God's inspiration all along was merely to return us to some original, blissfully-untroubled state of peace and transcendent silence, why bother to put us through this elaborately-complex evolutionary hoax to begin with? In fact, why bother to "wake up" at all if the point is simply to return to a dreamless or luminous sleep?

If, then, as this Agenda has suggested from the beginning, there is another purpose and intention behind the Divine's evolutionary will to be; and if, as suggested in those same seed passages, the secret behind this will to be is the Self-experience and expression of a divine delight of Being; and if the spontaneous nature inherent in this delight of Being is to freely give and share its Self utterly and without reserve, in essence equating the will to be with the will to love; and if, in this context, the universe is its garden, playground and field of Self-expression, in which and through which to end-lessly discover, experience and express that love and delight forever, like a child playing hide-and-seek with Her Self—pretending at first not to know who or where She is, pretending not to be free—so that She can experience the utter joy and surprise of Self-rediscov-ery through progressively-more-conscious forms and instruments of consciousness capable of containing, communicating and shar-ing that delight in ever-expanding spirals of oneness; then all of our present spiritual goals, realizations and powers need to defer them-selves to this core goal, joining together in an evolutionary con-spiracy to midwife the delivery of this child: Delight.

In which case, peace, silence and the states of inner poise, clar-ity and transparence which they confer on us, are no longer realiza-tions turned exclusively inward on themselves, but rather serve in a larger evolutionary context. In other words, while the disciplined development of such qualities and capacities is critical to our con-scious unfolding—silencing our monkey-minds; stilling our nerves, our restless vitalistic and emotional natures; infusing an imperturb-able poise into the very cells of our being—we must take care not to fall into the trap which would merely use these gifts to buffer and shield us from the transformational challenges of life, effec-tively reducing them to negative applications.

For if we simply use peace to avoid, numb or neutralize pain rather than face, heal and harmonize it at its source; if we attain inner silence merely to deafen ourselves to the cries of the world within and around us; if we use the inner centeredness of peace and silence as a hole in which to retreat rather than an unshakeable grounded poise from which to more consciously, courageously, effectively and practically respond to the accelerating crises and presenting symptoms threatening our terrestrial web of life; then we squander their evolutionary potentials, leaving them as half-way realizations, missing, this Agenda asserts, the whole point, punchline and plot of the Matter.

In fact, by pursuing these inner states as fixed spiritual goals rather than essential evolutionary means, we effectively disempower ourselves as transitional beings, abandoning, I believe, our creative destiny and that of the universe we carry forward with us; condemning ourselves to the path of transcendence rather than transformation; unwittingly building ourselves into a negative existential corner that, in its nihilistic extremes, lands us back in the Void; pointing us toward the austere summits of the monastery as spirituality's ultimate high-point and conclusion in a process that effectively rejects Life as an obstacle, distraction or contaminant to some inner or transcendent Truth; reducing the meaning of Life (if we cut through the rhetoric, mystique and esoterics) to a painful interlude, terminal illness and ordeal that we must bear with until Death forecloses, relieving us finally of our Illusion.

On the other hand, if we would reclaim and redefine Life as an as-yet unfulfilled but not unfulfillable Story, then we must heal the egoic split-vision that divorced peace from power; beginning to practice an evolutionary application of peace that reverses its present gravitational bias; avoiding the luminous blindspot that would turn peace into a spiritualized version of the ego's primal reflex to withdraw, retreat and contract. In other words, in the process of silencing our mental chatter-box, stilling our hyper-active nervous systems, freeing ourselves from the egoic addictions and attachments that keep us imprisoned in our superficial realities and values, we must simultaneously learn to detach ourselves from our detachments. Otherwise we risk trading materialistic addictions for spiritual ones, supporting a profounder habit and inner co-dependency whose "highs," from an evolution-of-consciousness perspective, keep us just as firmly hooked in their heights; setting us up for spiritual "withdrawal symptoms" that make it more and more difficult to descend, return to, affirm or function in material realities and bodies.

The evolutionary role and purpose of peace, then, is to provide us a more stable platform, equilibrium and center from which to heroically bear the influx of unprecedented power accompanying a next principle of Being; creating the receptive conditions and transparence for us to integrate, incorporate and contain a power that would shatter present ego-bound forms, vessels and systems. In other words, by infusing in cells and selves a *material* peace that stills all resistances, quells all fear, we expand present containment thresholds and tolerances toward frictionless clarity; gradually releasing ourselves layer by layer from the once-protective reflex to contract; eventually freeing ourselves from the egoic die of rigid mind-based forms to uniquely fluid-yet-physical figures of consciousness capable of breathing through the brittleness and contractions of the finite to birth the infinite ensouled in their core.

For what is pain, after all, but the experience of an experience whose intensity exceeds present system thresholds and capacities to contain it? In which case, the whole point and purpose of evolution is to prepare us through a progressive egolessness to receive the experience of Being as that Being experiences Itself, transforming this evolving universe into a conscious delivery system for delight through ego-free instruments capable of matching and harmonizing an intensity that intensifies to infinity...

...Which is why we do not greedily grab for it or try to force it into our own ignorant, ego-driven timetables, but rather learn to allow the wisdom and grace that in-forms that Power to guide us; revealing what we need to do and un-do, what we need to ask for and what we need to surrender. Our work as a transitional species, then, begins not by an adolescent impatience to seize the evolutionary goodies and *siddhis*, but by a humble self-giving: calling into the successive layers of our being a dynamic peace, poise and clarity; consciously plowing the egoic ground; offering up oneself in preparation to receive that experience of OneSelf for which we must change ourselves completely to receive/become it. For, as we continue to learn through our existential finger-burning, that which is truly all-creative, all-delightful, all-one in the Divine translates through ego as pain or, at best, flickering pleasures that tantalize but never fulfill.

It is from this perspective, then, that we must gear ourselves down for the work ahead; rolling up our sleeves to front pressing realities; accepting rather than fleeing from our species-level responsibilities; transposing static spiritual goals to dynamic evolutionary means; redirecting wisdoms previously turned toward nirvanic escape into elegantly-practical earthy applications; breaking through our gravities to actually begin formulating, adapting and adopting an Evolutionary Agenda for the Third Millennium; resolutely taking the mutational steps to consciously bridge ourselves forward; building in the process a true evolutionary trust and terrestrial collaboration with our future selves.

For at this unique turning point where the very meaning and measure of survival itself changes, we cannot save half a world, half a reality, half a person, choosing inner over outer or vice versa, without losing the *whole* thing.

SIX

PHASED METAMORPHOSIS

A TRANS-HUMAN APPROACH
TO THE THIRD MILLENNIUM

Each stage of consciousness in the onward mutational progression of our humanity is both a growth and flowering of its own unique seed-*dharma* and destiny[1] as well as the seed carrier for the next stage and species. In other words, the archetypal flowering of a species is not an end in itself. In fact, its completion and fulfillment lies in the successful transmission of new seeds, setting forth the promise for what is still to come. In which case, returning to our evolving evolutionary nomenclature, *Homo egoicus* is both the full-flowering of the egoic principle expressed through mentalized life forms, as well as the carapace, seed and bud for our successive trans-human species.

Each future phase of our evolutionary unfolding, then, is intimately budded in the previous emergence: *transitionalis* breaking

---

1. "Destiny" is defined here as the potential consciousness/power already *in*volved in the proto-conscious core DNA of each evolving being, species, genus, order, principle and cycle. In which case, each evolute operates within multiple macro and micro destinies, gravities and potentials at the same time, the more complex and highly-evolved the form, the more complex the web of destinies and ecology of consciousness. As humans approaching the threshold of a conscious mutation, then, we are simultaneously struggling to work through cumulative evolutionary residue as well as fulfill unresolved cellular, personal and species-level destinies.

through the tenacious night-blooming *egoicus; holisticus* and its in-termediaries unfurling more gracefully following the intense cycle, season and brief blossoming of *transitionalis;* leading finally to our more transparent dawn-blooming species that not only grow to-ward the sun but progressively manifest it in terrestrial forms.

Goals, Expectations and Scope for a Millennial Agenda

In this context, the attempt to draft an Evolutionary Agenda for our emerging millennium challenges us to keep our goals and expecta-tions honest: in touch with real-time terrestrial realities and the pressing questions and urgencies these realities raise; humbling and tempering that mental reflex in us which continues to look for final answers and results, setting us up for static one-shot revela-tions and panaceas, spiritual or technological. For only by fulfilling the vision and possibility seeded in each metamorphic moment can we open the evolutionary door to our emerging future and fu-ture selves.

The clearer we frame our evolutionary questions, then, the clearer we understand not only what it is that we need to under-stand but what we need to become; learning in the process to iden-tify and distinguish real needs from egoic counterfeits or artificially-induced dependencies.

ᶓ

Mindful of the fact that the subject matter of this inquiry and Agenda is life and consciousness—which, as living experience in-separable from ourselves, changes by the very act of living it—then we are not merely evolutionary observers but research subjects as well, coloring and co-creating the very experiences and events we witness. As such, our subject matter behaves like a moving target, presenting us with a unique exercise where both research material *and* researcher are evolving variables. Hence, the need to keep an eye on the observer and patterns of observing as well as that which is observed; monitoring ourselves as well as the reality-fields we inhabit; continuously updating, revising, editing and re-synthesizing our data, interpretations and directions accordingly.

In this two-way reality, then, what we call evolutionary change proceeds not only via objective physical and bio-chemical processes, but through subjective perception and interaction; shifting in manifest degrees from barely-visible subtleties to noticeable concreteness relative to

- pattern duration (i.e., Time's "objective" densification and gravity-making, older patterns gathering more mass); as well as
- ongoing evolutionary refinements in eyesight and I-sight (i.e., the successive upgrades and integrating capacities of our "subjective" receiving apparatus through which we tune in the multi-band vibrational frequency of Being).

In which case, the world that our cave-dwelling ancestors saw was not merely different from ours by virtue of geological or ecological conditions but was in fact a different reality because of subsequent shifts in hominid consciousness which literally altered sensory, perceptual, conceptual and cognitive experience.

This interactive nature of what we call "Reality" suggests that seeing is not merely a passive witness phenomenon but an active and creative one, reminding the skeptic in us that proof is not just a matter of "seeing is believing." For, conversely, we also auto-suggestively see what we believe or have been conditioned to believe/disbelieve, particularly if those beliefs (and their negative counterpart doubts) carry the gravitational sanctity, certitude and mass of Time.

With this perspective, then, aware that we are attempting to sketch the outline for a provisional Evolutionary Agenda designed to catalyze rather than proselytize, let us set realistic objectives: establishing agreements, ground-rules, guidelines and coordinates so we don't drift amorphously into abstraction or gravitate into catechism; clarifying limits and boundaries so expectations don't exceed the scope of such an exercise.

The straightforward goal and purpose of this Evolutionary Agenda is the transformation of terrestrial reality through a corresponding transformation of terrestrial consciousness; or, transcribed in evolutionized spiritual terms, the progressive divinization of Matter. Implicit in this primary goal is the successful passage of our species and planet through its metamorphic transition and series of transitions with the minimum of trauma and the maximum of grace.

The reduction of trauma, traumatic stress and shock, both at the individual and species level, is, as previous chapters have pointed out, directly proportional to the release of egoic resistance, rigidity and tension. And conversely, the movement to maximize grace corresponds to our willingness to adapt and incorporate the post-egoic art of letting go: of consciously breathing through the intensity of the contractions; effectively widening and expanding one's capacity to bear and bear with; retraining our genetic reflex to go with rather than against the evolutionary flow; replacing the bias to contract (the clenched fist) with a will to trust and open; fearlessly releasing in the process an outflow of compassion, self-giving and gratitude that heals us of our egoic tightness as we learn to move toward the frictionless light-speed of Love.

To address these primary and corollary goals, however, we must avoid the either-or atavism that would trap us in absolutist thinking and approaches. In which case, this Agenda intends to break down its evolutionary goals and visions into successive interim goals, stages, timelines and processes. While these sub-goals and corresponding timeframes are not rigidly segmented from one another, in fact oftentimes overlapping or operating simultaneously like destinies within destinies, nevertheless, the creation of graduated goals recognizes that evolution is process: i.e., that the realization of primary goals is neither an all-at-once spiritual leap from ignorance to enlightenment nor an all-at-once evolutionary leap from present-state bodies, minds and consciousness into some Nietzschean superman; but rather a progressively integrated series of shifts, incremental mutations and micro-bursts, individual and collective, leading eventually to more dramatic critical-mass combustion and emergent transformational forms.

The caterpillar, after all, doesn't simply morph into the butterfly, but enters into its chrysalis where it undergoes its radical metamorphosis in distinct phase changes, in effect dissolving past forms, systems and structures into protean stew in order for them to be creatively refashioned into something quite other than the previous sum of its parts. Similarly, our species and its collective institutions and societal forms must prepare for an extended metamorphic transition; allowing the inseparably-conjoined processes of destruction and creation, dissolution and resolution, breakdown and breakthrough, to proceed at their own pace; guided by the same wisdom that knows better than the caterpillar how quickly we can actually change, the alchemic process by which we can change, and the interim steps that need to be taken to assure the successful survival of the whole through the passage from larva to pupa to imago.

In which case, we need to expose that tendency in us which unconsciously lumps and confuses everything together, seeking/expecting one all-purpose formula, outcome, methodology or discipline to get us from our generic humanity to some spiritually-realized end-product. For this fatally-flawed confusion, distorting a priori the way the exercise is framed, sets us up for failure. In fact, if we explore this self-defeating expectation to its origins, I believe we will discover that core egoic bias operating beneath our conscious threshold, reading from its negatively-conditioned script, putting the words in our mouth, the doubts in our mind, before we even realize we have a choice: in this case, voicing itself in terms of "if I can't have it, see it, grasp it *now*, it doesn't exist."

To counter this fallacious yet deeply-engrained dialectic at the outset, then, is critical if we are to design an Evolutionary Agenda modeled on metamorphically-phased change rather than instant whack-on-the-head spiritual enlightenment or technology-driven social engineering; in effect, applying equally the concept of relativity reserved for matters of physics to matters of metaphysics, revising in the process the absolute and undifferentiated status of "God-realized" which we confer on spiritually evolved members of our species to "*relatively* God-realized," recognizing that the realization of God in the evolutionary sense is an infinite venture/adventure.

Evolutionizing Time

This change-over in paradigmatic models for change itself, adjusting the perception of Time into evolutionary rather than merely historical or Greenwich-based coefficients, is essential in our approach to this Agenda, establishing a new foundation and perch in Time from which to perceive and prioritize progressively-evolving goals and sub-agendas.

This "evolutionization" of time is an especially difficult psychological shift for our species, particularly its culturally-contagious American variety raised on fast foods, fast cars and quick fixes, conditioned like addicts to the need for speed — for instant gratification, instant proof, and its inner equivalent, instant realization. To effectively address this aspect of our trans-human shift, then, working through its subconscious conditioning, I believe we must elevate the way we conceptualize and measure time itself to a species-level goal of this Agenda; recasting it into a larger evolutionary context, relevance and reality; recalibrating perspectives to acknowledge the dimensional movement of multiple times and wave patterns ticking simultaneously within one another, atomic and molecular frequencies vibrating within the slower measures of human time, historical cycles spinning within the vaster rhythms of terrestrial and cosmological time, each in this coinciding moment approaching individual and convergent criticality.

In this expanding framework of time, we actually need to gear things down, working through our adolescent impatience for immediate answers, results, proof; stilling our hyperactive nervous systems, individual and cultural; freeing ourselves from our ulcer-generating expectations and demands for final maps and manuals, finished plans and products; exposing that impulse in us which, despite our cries for freedom, wants to be led, told what to do, intimidated by the awesome responsibility of actually fronting the unknown.

To meet this new sense and responsibility of time, then, we need to effectively slow ourselves down within if we would consciously match and respond to the acceleration and urgency of things without. For in the relativity-paradox of time, this thesis suggests, the more unhurried our inner rhythm, the more swift and efficient our outer movements: minimizing friction and meltdown; breathing through our hyper-ventilations and tendencies to seize up; operating from a truer center in time-space that sees more effortlessly, egolessly and clearly what is to be done and how to do it; in effect changing things not only by the *way* in which we approach them but the *time* in which we approach them.

In this more holistic approach to time, inversely synchronizing subjective and objective timings, we must reset our psychological clocks, switching from stop-watch measures and polarities (i.e., utopian/doomsday scenarios at the stroke of midnight) to phased metamorphosis; humbling our strategy to that of a marathoner; developing the critical trans-human quality of perseverance; breathing in larger cycles; pacing our evolutionary change in terms of transitional steps, stages, synapses; redefining ourselves not as a single fixed species but a series of unfolding sub-species, each with its own unique sub-agendas, each running its own lap, shorter or longer-strided, in this human relay race, passing the baton of consciousness in a micro-burst to that next forerunner who is still none other than ourselves.

From this evolutionary vantage point in Time, then, we can begin to read like tea leaves the larger patterns and possibilities latent in present embryonic global phenomena; registering, interpreting and revaluing the spontaneous emergence of countless personal and community-based experiments bursting out all over the planet not merely as isolated or aberrant historical events but as the initial outgrowth and manifestation of a previously-*involved* evolutionary principle through a nascent trans-human being. In this context, the resurgent interest in esoteric spiritual traditions and the wisdom of more ancient cultures is not an indicator of a return to the past, past patterns or ways of thinking, but rather of a species-level refocusing on Consciousness: a review (as distinct from repetition) of our previous spiritual and philosophical inquiries, methodologies and realizations in the same way that one would review previous research before exploring new scenarios, original hypotheses and creative directions; integrating and incorporating still-relevant ancient knowledge, reminders and techniques as a base, benchmark and platform from which to spring forward into undiscovered fields of knowing and being.

In effect, then, each of our emerging trans- and post-human species has its own unique mission, destiny, role, rhythm of unfolding and corresponding evolutionary sub-agenda to fulfill in the larger spectrum of our metamorphic passage. In which case, to realistically develop an Evolutionary Agenda in millennial time-cycles, we must consciously frame the experiment in terms of a series of trans-species agendas, formatting them within their respective mutational timeframes rather than a single one-size-fits-all evolutionary formulation. For through this attempt to clarify and classify our onward mutation of consciousness into a series of distinct yet interconnected stages and phase-changes, we avoid the blindspot which reflexively superimposes expectations that actually belong to a far more distant end-stage onto a more immediate interim one.

In other words, if the elimination of money as a measure of value and means of exchange is (as we shall take up in a future chapter) one of this Agenda's millennial goals, we must avoid the tendency to measure its practicality or viability in terms of overnight timeframes for success or failure. For it is this false measurement, conditioned by our shortsighted approach to time and change, that leads us to scoff at such a proposition, dismissing it prima facie as ridiculous prior to even submitting it to a serious and unprejudiced research. If, on the other hand, we phase our goals rather than framing them in all-or-nothing expectations, setting less ambitious targets and standards for *H. transitionalis* than for a more time-distant holistic humanity no longer dominated by egoic values and behaviors, we pace change into more manageable and achievable increments, matching outer shifts to inner mutations and potentialities.

Identifying and consequently liberating ourselves, then, from this kneejerk judgment which overlays short-term historical expectations on long-term evolutionary pattern-changes is essential if we are to get past the "if I can't see it *now*, it's unreal or unreachable" variety of reality assessment and planning; reclaiming in that recognition the power we unconsciously give away to that initial, predictable reaction which (in the case of a post-monetary society, for example) characterizes and stigmatizes such possibilities as too utopian and unworkable, assuring us a massive breakdown in societal order, functioning, continuity, etc. etc. For by buying into such a dead-end dialectic, we effectively talk ourselves out of the possibility before legitimately exploring it, shutting the door based on historical proof (i.e., past failures), short-term expectations or simply what we assume to be "the nature of human nature."

A closer look, however, shifting reference points for the way and time in which we plan, define and measure "success," frees us from the grip of these arguments and assumptions; cutting through the rhetoric and reasoning which disproves a proposition purely based on past failures or the apparent incorrigibility of human nature: i.e., "This is the way it has always been, therefore, this is the way it will always be." For if we adopt an evolutionary perspective, evolution seems to suggest that precisely *because* it has never been, it will be.

In this larger, more methodical and integral approach to time, then, utilizing an evolutionary model that addresses change in assimilable degrees, ratcheting up the intensity relative to stress-thresholds rather than suddenly unleashing it in one massive fuse-blowing burst, we must take care not to impatiently demand millennial or century-level results in years or decades. For time like space has its vessels and containment thresholds. And forcing century-magnitude shifts into five-year plans would simply overload societal systems, producing the very Mad Max scenarios we fear in our jaded "I told you so" mindset. (In fact, for that egoic mindset, invested more in being right rather than being true, anticipating the negative like a vulture waiting for things to collapse, failure becomes a perverse form of success.)

In any case, evolution itself is speeding up, though we do not recognize it from our egoic reference point in time. This inability to perceive the acceleration of time parallels a more tangible spatial example, operating in the same way that looking out the window of a plane at the earth below does not give us a sense of moving faster than looking out a car at the passing scenery, creating the illusion of similar speeds even though the plane is traveling hundreds of miles an hour faster than the car. This cognitive phenomenon, I believe, points out the distortion of measuring time, speed, movement and reality relative to our present selves and senses.

By figurative analogy, then, what may take a century for present species-level consciousness to realize might have taken a thousand centuries for a pre-Einsteinian version of our humanity, just as it may only take a year for some future trans-human version. In fact, theoretically completing our progression, it may eventually take no time at all for a species whose consciousness is traveling at light-speed, i.e., in which there is no time gap between intention and re-alization, will and manifestation. If, then, evolution itself is accelerating, it would be counter-productive for us in our present ignorance to further stress system thresholds by arbitrarily attempting to make things go faster than the wisdom governing time's hyper-mechanics is already cycling.

By incorporating this "evolutionized" sense of time and timing, then, we effectively learn the critical trans-species art of turning time into an ally rather than enemy, working with rather than against her, not forcing arbitrary shortsighted expectations on long-term evolutionary "projects." This new ground and background of time, then, provides us a more profound platform, context and incentive from which to forge our way forward; allowing ourselves the time-space, the breathing-room, to actually test premises and adapt applications as we go; form following function, function following consciousness in a genuine applied evolutionary research; each step building the bridge, strengthening the foundation for the next so that one day the possibilities that seemed so utterly impossible to *H. egoicus* become effortless and graceful realities; turning true because we have turned true along with them, working out our selves in the process of working out the world.

Applying this larger Time perspective to present-time terrestrial crises and urgencies, however, should not be egoically misinterpreted as a rationale to kick back and procrastinate. For if we continue to wait for some *deus ex machina*, spiritual or secular, to save us from ourselves—some final proof, verification or sanctification that ordains us as transitional beings, giving us permission to finally risk seizing the initiative in our evolutionary destiny—it may be too late for terrestrial life-support systems to recuperate, passing their point of no return. Now, after all, *is* the only moment before us.

What remains, then, is simply to call our own evolutionary bluff. But to call it wisely, respectfully, compassionately and perseveringly so that we don't unnecessarily add to the breakdown or burn ourselves out in one do-or-die burst. In which case, if we can establish a more comprehensive milieu for our species and this unprecedented hour in earth-time, setting the accelerating madness of our present humanity in the context of a wider sense of who we are and where we are heading, even if that vision is still imprecise and "under construction," we build in a trans-human perspective that helps us call that formidable, debilitating bluff; providing ourselves a tool to leverage us from our ego-inherited shell and spell; reminding ourselves that we are not defined by what we knew and were but what we are yet to become.

Trans-Human Agendas:
Metamorphosing from Myth to Matter

Approaching our future and future selves, this chapter suggests, is a consciousness-based exercise in phased metamorphosis, beginning from the near and working outward (or inward) toward the far. In this regard, the hypotheses, premises and proposals contained in this section resemble the developmental structure of an embryo: that is, a conceptual form still in its generic "stem cell" stage of formation, where initial emphasis is on prototypal concepts, holistic context and synoptic overview rather than differentiated line-item details—strengthening the integrity and viability of the embryonic whole before prematurely struggling to unfold the bud, dissect or tear apart the petals. Consistent with this understanding, the intent here is

- to draft a provisional outline for millennial-based, species-level change that subsequent chapters and future research can more fairly develop, test, modify and refine;
- to fit pieces together in such a way that the evolutionary puzzle begins to take shape, interpreting presently-chaotic or apparently-senseless events through a larger, more embracing sense;
- to provide an evolutionary context which invites the reader to divine for herself a more coherent pattern in millennial time-space; encouraging and empowering her to fill in the blanks through personal exploration, inquiry and activism, tapping into the vast and vastly-accessible outpouring of cutting-edge references, research and resources.

Working forward, then, from present to future, from near to far, let us begin our inquiry into the mutational shift from *H. egoicus* to *transitionalis.*

Homo Transitionalis

The transitional humanity which this Agenda has called *Homo transitionalis* represents the first attempt by an earth-based species in 13.7 billion years of evolutionary time (at current cosmo-chronological estimates) to consciously will its own mutation; branching, however timidly and awkwardly, by choice rather than mechanism.

As indicated in the previous chapter, this initial trans-species shift from full-blown Ego Man toward a post-egoic person is at once the briefest, most critical and most wrenching. For it presents us with the unprecedented departure from the conditioning, orientation and values of an entire egoic evolutionary cycle; in effect, stripping us of our existential security blanket; extricating us from the gravity and ideological habit-patterns which establish our sense of "the way it is." At the same time, it faces us with our own extinction if we fall back into the pull of those egoic patterns; leaving us damned if struggle to break free of them but even more damned if we succumb to them. In which case, ducking or denying the accumulating crises which greet us at the threshold of this twenty-first century in effect only increases their power and pain.

With one hand, then, drawing us forward even as it holds our feet to the fire, reminding us in painfully unmistakable personal and planetary terms why we must consciously transition to a new species; while the other hand pulls us back, ever-more-desperately clinging to us, tightening its grip, fighting for its egoic life to preserve what we have been and known, *transitionalis* is caught in the evolutionary cross-fire—literally as well as figuratively torn by the tension of conflicting gravities and magnetisms; drawn forward by evolution, pulled back by devolution; light wrestling to free itself from its matrix, from some fathomless egoic black hole inexorably sucking life and being back to death and unbeing; forces past clashing with forces present and future in a titanic terrestrial collision.

If, as this Agenda proposes, this is more than just metaphor, if in fact this is where myth begins to metamorphose and manifest in matter, then we are not just *witnessing* our own mutation but, like it or not, are pressed to *participate* in it. Or, more crudely put, to choose evolutionary sides. For in this moment, there are no evolutionary bystanders, no neutrals, no exemptions or immunities: A moment, finally, where what does not move forward falls back— where we can no longer simply tread water, sustaining an egoic lifestyle that is in reality (as future chapters shall develop) a deathstyle, a death sentence for ourselves and our planet.

Transitionalis, then, is that stage of our humanity, back against the wall, where we've run out of wiggle room, scapegoats, excuses and denials; leaving us like the Emperor looking at himself through the mirror of his own child-self, divested of his vainglorious illusions and mental pretensions, seeing his naked reflection behind all the formidable egoic armor, gilding and gilt, religious or technological. "No clothes," he hears the child laughing. No clothes, the chilling phrase re-echoes in his mind, his frantically spinning ego-scripted mind still hoping somehow to conjure another mask, to buy its way out of its utter predicament, forestalling the inevitable. But all the King sees, no matter how hard he shuts his eyes, is that child smiling innocently, sweetly but mercilessly, pointing out the one thing our ego at all costs doesn't want to see: Its own fallibility, vulnerability, mortality.

"No clothes, no close, open," the child chides him, chides us now, reminding us in inescapable planetary terms of that choice we have waited nearly fourteen billion years to make: A choice where to hesitate, to stubbornly resist or reflexively contract, simply prolongs and increases the agony and angst, feeding the friction and stress-levels as we begin to red-line, reaching maximum tolerance as a sentient species. This, then, is the conscious choice that lies before us, initiating us on the path of a new species—a transitional sub-species that does not yet know the road it must travel but unequivocally knows it must risk the journey, replacing in the process its egoic vessel with a truer one. For our vessels as well as the bridges behind us are burning, the evolutionary child points out, beckoning us through the flames. "No clothes, no close, open," she repeats her refrain, inviting us to embark on the Adventure.

"No," *egoicus* cries out in pain, retreating to its core genetic script, still invested in its cloak of nothingness, willing to defend that nothingness to the death. "Yes," *transitionalis*, finally says, calling the Emperor's bluff, heroically choosing to change, letting the unbearable weight of a cloak-that-never-was fall, releasing us gradually from a gravity of death to a gravity of love that grows lighter as we give ourselves to its embrace.

ξ

It is the unique and awesome role, then, of this emergent trans-humanity to serve as a vanguard for our future, building a bridgehead and base camp for the onward mutation of our species. Practically speaking, its primary mission is nothing less than fronting and reversing the present suicidal course of *H. egoicus*; effectively winning ourselves and planet the time to heal and recuperate before earth's fragile ecology, despite its extraordinary resilience, reaches terminal devolutionary limits, unable to recover quality of life even if it can somehow survive at a more primitive or primal level. In other words, *transitionalis*, while aware that we must begin to work on core transformational issues, must keep itself humbly focused on earth—on identifying, prioritizing and *addressing* the most urgent and life-threatening of our planetary symptoms, practicing what an earlier chapter referred to as evolutionary triage.

Such a Herculean task demands that we cut through our rhetoric to actually stabilize planetary life-systems and relieve psycho-cellular stress levels; implementing, rather than merely sermonizing about the need for, more consciously viable and sustainable lifestyles; leveraging ourselves from the inertia of passive agreement to personal action; breaking through the mesmerism of our false wisdoms—our Enron-guided, profit-at-any-cost counsels—that would endlessly debate or deny the urgency of our crises even as the Antarctic melts, the school budgets burn, the wilderness recedes and the pathogens and terrorists continue to multiply, developing new resistant strains, microbial or human, in response to our upgraded antibiotic arsenals and close-fisted approach-to-solutions, military or pharmaceutical.

It is this willingness to confront and overcome the gravity of one's personal and collective patterns, accepting that the evolutionary buck stops here, now, with us, I believe, that distinguishes a truly trans-humanity from its egoic counterfeits and New Age pretenders, marking the material branching point and authentic departure from Ego Man's telltale "do as I say but not as I do" methodology. For what constitutes our actual sub-species shift is not simply the recognition of what needs to be done, but the will and determination to do it, regardless of the risk and egoic sacrifice; prioritized like a woman in labor on the birth to come and the well-being of the child; willing to forgo our temporal pleasure-patterns and comfort-zones, accepting and enduring the inconveniences and ordeals in the light of what is at stake. In other words, collaborating with our destiny rather than simply submitting to our fate.

The application of a post-egoic survival strategy, sustainability and evolutionary activism (which future chapters shall explore in greater depth), I believe, defines the primary scope and mission of *transitionalis*. In the present overview, then, what are the broad lines and timeframes through which *transitionalis* establishes its niche in the emerging spectrum of consciousness?

To meaningfully explore the timeline of *transitionalis*, we must incorporate the overlapping period of its emergence through and coexistence with *egoicus*. For new species, as we have seen, do not emerge ready-made. In the case, then, of *transitionalis*, the initial influx of a new consciousness in existing human forms—effectively a "takeover from within"—began to manifest in the 1960s. For it was that creative moment in history that saw a radical infusion of new reality-perceptions and values, unleashing human consciousness from its straightjacket uniformity, marking—despite its detractors who still cynically dismiss it as self-infatuated naïveté, irrelevant aberration or resurgent paganism—an irreversible global (as distinct from local, national or cultural) evolutionary phenomenon.

This phenomenon expressed itself with extraordinary swiftness and unprecedented diversity, proliferating through a multidimensional explosion of experiences and events that saw the emergence of hippies, mind-altering drugs, music, art; the morphing of clothes, fashions, diets, hairstyles, values; the inner assault upon the bastions of Western empiricism through an alien invasion of gurus and monks armed with incense and ragas, mystical texts and Sanskrit mantras, at the same time that whole generations of youth were taking to the streets in Berkeley and Paris, Washington and Prague; rising up against the Bastille of Western norms and lemming-like social patterns; self-organizing into a formidable wave-force that eventually broke the Viet Nam War, barrier-breaking across the landscape in the movements for civil rights, free speech, gender equality, economic justice, demilitarization; opening a Pandora's box of human potentials at the same moment that we saw ourselves for the first time from space as a single, blue, borderless planet, elegantly set like a precious and irreplaceable jewel that belonged to no one, no nation, no species.

It is the magnitude, scope and simultaneity, then, of this phenomenon that, I believe, distinguishes and qualifies it as a genuine species-level mutational shift, even if it appeared to wither and fade, checked, obscured and resisted through successive backlashes and reactionary counter-waves from the egoic right during the 1970s, 80s and 90s. For what often presents itself on the surface as retreat or defeat is, from an evolutionary perspective, a strategic in-gathering of energies, incubating, integrating and regrouping for a more conscious and sustainable resurgence. It is in this sense, then, that we must never underestimate the power-to-change locked within each one of us, nor measure what is possible by the standards of what is impossible.

Moving back, then, into present time, I believe we have already lived through the emergent seed-phase of *transitionalis*, in effect acclimating and adjusting ourselves to it now over several decades. As a result, many of its initially-radical concepts, patterns and behaviors are no longer utterly unique or unheard-of (i.e., ecology, yoga classes, whole-system thinking, body-mind realities, organic farming, conflict resolution, etc.), incorporated, assimilated and blended into mainstream thought, culture and idioms. The fact, however, that these consciousness changes have already incarnated into noetic and terrestrial realities, taken up into our psychologies, medical practices and marketing techniques, by no means diminishes their importance in the larger scheme of things. In fact, this is how *transitionalis* leap-frogs us forward; consolidating and more consciously building off these evolving experiences and insights; strengthening our species-level base as we forge ahead.

The danger, however, in this assimilation process is that the ego, no longer able to simply overpower or block these emergent evolutionary insights and experiences, employs more subtle tactics, cleverly manipulating and claiming these experiences and insights as its own; turning them into new versions of old traps; distorting concepts such as globalization into expanded fields for egoic conquest and corporate dominion; utilizing emergent knowledge, media and technologies to enhance marketability and mesmerism, selling us into even more lethal patterns of consumption, apathy, despair and more consumption.

It is the role of *transitionalis*, then, in the urgent decades to come to see through this egoic power play, focusing its evolutionary activism not only on outer change and mechanisms but on the even more insidious vestiges of *egoicus* that we still blindly carry like a Trojan horse within ourselves. In other words, while we must agitate and legislate new economic, environmental and humanitarian-based laws, the real litmus test for *transitionalis* lies in humbly living those laws and policies from within outward, vibrationally transforming the worlds we inhabit by a force of *being*, not simply thinking. For the mind, after all, still remains largely an instrument of egoic conditioning and self-defense, designed to retain the supremacy of its regimes despite its transformational rhetoric.

ᘓ

Without quibbling over dates or details, it is clear that we cannot support present terrestrial trends—natural resource depletion, human consumption patterns, population expansion, societal destabilization and psychological stress levels—indefinitely. For the earth, despite its relative magnitude or the extraordinary magnitude of our ignorance, behaves like all cellular life-forms. If, then, we are on the terrestrial bubble, at the point where we begin to exceed biospheric and noetic integrity, i.e., the carrying-capacity and system threshold of our planet, it doesn't take a prophet to foresee that the next decades will either witness the pyrrhic victory of *egoicus*, stubbornly choreographing our doom; or the coming of age of *transitionalis*, providing our species a decisive reversal of direction and momentum from our twentieth century madness.

This hypothetical timeline for make-or-break mutational change, based more on evolutionary instinct and commonsense than hard scientific data (which, after all, is only as "hard" as our instruments and interpretations), operates from the evolutionary principle that, despite our egoic rhetoric and professed beliefs, we only change when the pain of resisting finally exceeds the fear and pain of change. It is not, then, through reason alone that *transitionalis* will convert *egoicus* (or the egoic residue still present in *transitionalis* itself). Because *egoicus*, despite its *sapient* mental appearances, is not governed by reason and rationality but by a far more primitive egoic guidance system.

In which case, the very denial systems, resistance to change and reflex to contract (which, this Agenda contends, constitute the core survival coding, ego-preservational instincts and pre-rational decisionmaking governing *egoicus*) are the same evolutionary devices that ironically orchestrate, facilitate and accelerate the changes they oppose. In other words, the very archaic blindness which has pushed us to the species-level brink and breaking-point creates the smelling-salt conditions that finally rouse us from our stupor, rescuing us from ourselves just in the evolutionary nick of time.

The transfer of power to *transitionalis*, then, by mid-twenty-first century, is not simply a pollyannish hope but a hardcore faith in a more profound Tao of Evolution: An evolutionary Tao where everything, even our ignorances and resistances, leads us unerringly to our truth in an elegantly simple biofeedback reality—a reality where the more we resist, the more painful the friction becomes, channeling us despite ourselves like a rat in a maze to finally find the way through our transition. One of the key lessons and adaptations, however, of this first trans-human transition is to learn to change willingly rather than through the unconscious mechanism of pain, collaborating consciously and eventually joyfully in future species-level mutations of our transformational journey.

Homo Polaris

While *transitionalis* represents the turn-around from our present gravity-driven course, addressing our most life-threatening terrestrial symptoms in order to stabilize psychological, cultural and ecological systems, I believe there are still intermediary trans-human species between *transitionalis* and the more radically-evolved *holisticus*. For the successful application of evolutionary triage, effectively winning us the survival time to actually recuperate, is itself an interim rather than end-goal—a clearing and preparatory stage for more positive-directed transformative processes, phases and forms.

In this context, expanding upon this Agenda's evolving evolutionary nomenclature and vision, it would seem that some interim species, linking us from our initial trans-humanity to a more luminously-guided holistic humanity, needs to bridge the gap. For once we have released ourselves from the crisis-management mode of *transitionalis* and its preoccupation with primarily negative issues, urgencies and damage-control, addressing symptoms and shadows that would kill us if we ignored them, we can begin to turn our conscious attention to more positive and creative directions, healing ourselves at more profound levels of our being that we couldn't address prior to stabilizing the patient. (It is, after all, premature to fantasize our future "spiritual" development as a species while we still blindly, schizophrenically pursue our abusive, ego-driven concept of "material" development and the devastating clear-cut pattern following in its wake.)

Pursuing this speculative exercise, then, this post-transitional, pre-holistic species could be called *Homo polaris*, its name derived from the northern polestar by which earlier versions of our race navigated unexplored seas. In which case, *H. polaris* represents that future humanity which has definitively refocused species-level goals, behavior and directions; decisively reoriented toward who and where we are heading; no longer preoccupied with the agenda of *transitionalis*, with mitigating the negative in its grosser, more destructive forms; freed finally to apply itself to working out the finer points of our residual unconsciousness, unfolding in the process our greater evolutionary potentials. While still bearing the imprint of its egoic origins and codings, then, *polaris* marks that species which is no longer simply at the turning-point but has actually made the turn, the balance of power definitively shifting toward a post-egoic person, vision and society.

In terms of its timeline,[2] this thesis suggests that the emergent overlap of *polaris* with *transitionalis* could predate the mid-twenty-first century, the second half of this century foreseeing the rapid transition to post-egoic values, orientations, perspectives and their corresponding urban, socio-economic and environmental forms. It

---

2. These projected evolutionary timelines, intended to provide a chronological overview for emergent trans-human species, should not be interpreted too rigidly or literally, as if they proceed single file in discrete, one-at-a-time stages. For both at the macro and micro level, we operate multidimensionally. In which case, as individuals, I believe we will experience and express a combination of these species-level states of conscious-

is critical, however, to remind ourselves that these external form-changes and decisionmaking patterns are not the result of linear, technology-driven progression and programming but rather the natural consequence and outer expression of an expanding inner consciousness: An evolution of consciousness at a stage where it can finally begin to determine its forms through a more conscious and *in*forming self-will rather than merely *con*forming to or perpetuating already-existing forms and patterns; expressing itself in more unitive, integrated plans and planning, manifesting a more profoundly compassionate, aesthetic and ecological principle and vision of being.

In this scenario, then, the primary scope and mission of *polaris* is equally balanced between inner and outer, spiritual and material. In fact, I believe it is with *polaris* and its more truly egalitarian perspective that we will see the shift away from this archaic spirit/matter dichotomy and its elitist world-view to a more holistic, embracing, post-egoic framework and terminology that rephrases "subject" and "object" matter in terms of consciousness and field of awareness. Once such a paradigm shift is firmly established, what we presently perceive and label as spiritual, mystical or miraculous powers and *siddhis* (associated with yogis, adepts, shamans or occultists) will gradually "democratize": no longer exclusively belonging to the Brahmins, acquired through closed-door initiations or harnessed through the strain of ascetic disci-

---

ness at the same time: the more highly evolved parts of our nature even now opening to and influenced by the consciousness equivalent of more time-distant species, the more obscure elements in us still dominated by our past, living out in oneself multiple selves, multiple stages of being, as we move toward becoming fully integrated beings. With this internal multiplicity, then, one can expect fluctuations of consciousness, pulled backward or drawn forward in time—one day, one hour, one moment, guided by *polaris*, inspired by *holisticus* or even the touch of our true psyche, the next mired once again in *egoicus, transitionalis* struggling through us to regain a more trustworthy center and ground of being.

plines, but progressively rooted in the very nature, norm and consciousness of the emergent species itself.

With *H. polaris*, then, I believe we will begin a more rhythmic and graceful phase of integrated growth; freed from the urgencies of a previous transition that demanded our primary attention; able to consolidate and build upon the post-egoic directions seeded by *transitionalis* as we simultaneously explore exponential inner change. In other words, designing new energy, transport and industrial infrastructures as an outgrowth of expanding cognitive insights, intuitive capacities and sensory range; liberating ourselves from the gravity of neo-stone age technologies (i.e., the top-heavy, mind-complicated, carbon-burning, resource-depleting and polluting engines of an egoic civilization and commerce) as we move toward that more harmonic society[3] which *Homo holisticus* and its successors portend.

This integrated inner-outer progression, however, does not simply translate in terms of collective and institutional change—the physical body of our societies—but in the progressive metamorphosis of our individual bodies as well. For through the release of inner potentials of consciousness and the subsequent release of previously-locked powers of love, openness and self-giving, we directly act upon deeper levels of transformation and bodily functioning; translating eventually into noticeable organic and cellular changes; manifesting not only in new patterns of thinking and behaving but new patterns of breathing and metabolism, systemic in-

---

3. Sri Aurobindo foresaw a future societal and collective progression paralleling our individual evolution of consciousness—a societal progression which fulfilled its *supra*mental possibilities in what he referred to as a "gnostic collectivity". This gnostic society and its corresponding post-egoic forms of relationship, self-organization and governance would, as I understand it, reflect and embody the unitive nature, dharma, freedom and spontaneous harmony coded in (to use the idiom of this Agenda) the very DNA of the supramentalized beings who comprise it.

tegrity and harmony—all of which in turn feed back into corresponding macro-changes: for example, implementing "lighter" agricultural methods, food sources and processing relative to more liberated, consciousness-based nutritional needs and methods of digestion.

Homo Holisticus

As we peer further into our future, details become hazier, more generalized, less precise, in the same way that Galileo's telescope could not match the focus, clarity or range of Hubble's. As explorers in consciousness, then, we are still at the neophyte stage, looking through a mental lens equivalent to that of our first astronomers, getting our first glimpse of stars and constellations of consciousness we didn't even know existed. As a result, our vision blurs as we seek to penetrate beyond the obscurities of *egoicus* and the threshold of *transitionalis*. Nevertheless, we can at least begin to acknowledge and affirm the existence of distant galaxies, of post-mental ways of knowing and being, even if we cannot yet glimpse the inner solar systems and life-forms which inhabit them and us.

In which case, even though our attempt to project beyond *polaris* becomes a more abstract and speculative affair, it still serves to round out our arc of human consciousness; completing our progression of mind-based evolution to its fullest term preceding the radical synapse to a post-egoic, *supra*mental cycle of being and becoming. According to this Agenda's hypothesis, then, *Homo holisticus* fulfills our present genus and spectrum of trans-human being, representing the true and mature version of *Homo sapiens* as wisdom-based mental beings.

The movement from *H. polaris* to *holisticus* shifts the pendulum of consciousness from intermediate to core levels of transformation, working at our pre-rational roots to release egoic residue from the deeper subconscious caves and cellular layers where ego still resides and presides over our primal genetic script, gravitational entropy and devolutionary behavior patterns. It is this holistic humanity, then, which shifts decisively from the emergent intelligence of *polaris* (which, despite its expanding intuitive capacities, nevertheless remains mixed and vulnerable to subtle egoic distortions) to what Sri Aurobindo called a "mind of light"—which, as I interpret it here, represents a mentalized instrument of knowing cleared of all shadow, friction and discord, all egoic bias, obscurity and influence; coming as close as one can come to transparent, ego-free reception, transmission and communication of experience through a lens still formed via egoic evolution.

Such a holistic-visioned species, possessed of a mind poised at the luminous threshold of a wholly new evolutionary principle and power, can begin to more effectively collaborate with and direct that next principle toward the complete transformation of Matter and material being; successively opening and surrendering any last vestiges of egoic control to that supramental Power which exceeds it; inviting in that wisdom-informed Power to permeate our beings layer by layer from the highest heights all the way down to cells of the body; letting it progressively reintegrate, harmonize and align the various planes and dimensions of our selves—thought, will, emotions, sensations, corporeality—in one conscious continuum around a new egoless center; simultaneously calling forth that same evolutionary Power to actively transform through us the collective consciousness, societal forms and institutions around us.

While it is beyond the scope of this inquiry to provide a precise timeline for *holisticus* (for how can we possibly predict the speed of future consciousness changes from present means and measures?), I believe it can begin to emerge through a mature *polaris* by the twenty-second century; gathering exponential speed as it flowers; manifesting more and more physically through the succeeding centuries via new organic ways of being at the individual as well as geo-collective level; pushing back the entropic inevitability and gravity of death as egoic evolution's ultimate law; bringing a new consciousness, joy and sense of wholeness no longer restricted to inner or transcendent realities but opened finally to bodies and cellves, regardless of scale or magnitude…

…Spiraling outward and inward, integrating cellular wholes within individual bodily wholes, harmonizing bodily wholes like cells in the wider whole of our planetary body, embracing the whole of our planetary body like a macro-cell in the body of the Divine; cycling toward a point of accelerating conscious mass where Evolution Herself finally breaks out of its egoic orbit, breaking through the egoic eggshell, spiraling freely into ever-wider and more conscious wholes; no longer motivated or leveraged by pain; no longer oscillating from pain to pleasure, shadow to light, but drawn forward in shadowless progressions from light to greater light, joy to greater joy, life to greater life, love to greater love in an ever-unfolding embrace of oneness; inspired solely by that Self-existent child-delight of Being that has in fact always been there, here, moving us from the beginningless beginning of this Story toward the fulfillment of its endless end which begins with…

Psyche Materialis

With the emergence, development and maturation of *Homo holisticus*, then, seeing us through mid-millennium, the butterfly species waiting in the wings prepares itself for its manifestation from myth to matter; slipping gracefully forth in its own time and timing as that first genus and species—*Psyche materialis*—of a whole new post-egoic order and evolutionary cycle: A post-human, supramental being at once truly individualized yet fully and materially conscious of its indivisible oneness with all; not only centered around its true soul and psychic self but integrally reflecting and radiating that core conscious self at every level of being.

In other words, a life-form no longer generated through ego, egoic conditioning, instrumentations, formational processes or forms even in their most sublime versions; self-formed in a wholly different way that no longer requires intermediary means, methods or midwives; embodying a fully-conscious presence in a fully-conscious body, where there is no longer division between inner transparence and outer translation, between wisdom and will, peace and power, intention and realization; moving at the effortless light-speed of Grace—the speed of Being, in which there is no longer the friction of struggle or strife to reach, become or possess that which one already *is*...

...A truly new being in a truly new body, no longer subject to the egoic laws of gravity, doubt or death, materializing Love and all our heart's innermost dreams and possibilities into tangible, embraceable, terrestrial terms: in a transformed Matter where He and She meet and reunite in an all-creative S/He, completing the circuit, merging into something/some*One* utterly other than the previous sum of its parts, birthing that secret child for whom all evolution has been a pretext and play of Self-discovery.

SEVEN

EVOLUTIONIZING HUMANITY FOR THE TWENTY-FIRST CENTURY

Moving from millennial conceptualizing to actually begin practicing an applied evolutionary research, in effect synapsing from words and theories to actions, is nothing less than taking the first steps as a species in its own mutation of consciousness. Toward this goal, the succeeding chapters of this work will focus on the phase-one transition of our metamorphosis as we simultaneously struggle to deprogram from our egocentric conditioning and reprogram a more holistically-viable alternative. This first-phase process, then, will revisit the application of evolutionary triage, attempting to address and develop more integrally-sustainable survival strategies for our species through an emergent evolutionary activism.

While some of the perspectives, premises and proposals already set forth in previous chapters help build in a support structure for the evolutionary bridge this Agenda is attempting to forge, nevertheless, some of the forthcoming premises and proposals will still read like utopian fiction. In this context, it is important to remind ourselves that:

- We must avoid the reflex to impatiently judge projects and programs of an evolutionary scale and proportion by the myopic timeframes and expectations of the ego.
- We must understand and anticipate that Mind itself—threatened at its roots by the prospects of being dethroned

by a greater evolutionary principle, power of knowing and being—will instinctively react from a self-preservational defense mechanism, either passively retreating from or aggressively rejecting a priori such research and exploration, declaring it too dangerous or too absurd, reclaiming our allegiance with a subconscious litany of all that can possibly go wrong if we dare to leave the safety of its borders.

The Evolutionary Art of Conscious Choice

One of the first skills that we must develop, then, in this attempt to evolutionize ourselves in preparation for the intensities and challenges of the twenty-first century is the art of conscious choice: of actually *choosing* rather than simply abdicating to the mechanics of our habit-patterns or that unconscious default doubt with which the ego habitually greets all new ideas and experiences. This liberating skill—initiating us into a more conscious, effective and responsible level of decisionmaking—begins by learning to identify that invisible reflex in us that automatically defers to habit or doubt. For by catching it/us in the act, we deflate the controlling power of the pattern, turning doubt back on itself, in effect, using doubt's own all-convincing negative force to neutralize itself.

As a species, then, at the launching stage of unprecedented evolutionary change, it is imperative that we offset and replace this archaic reflex which, without our conscious consent, immediately opposes such change by placing our unquestioned faith in the negative or repetitive. For by elevating doubt to our core belief, we unwittingly disempower ourselves, dooming our evolutionary hypotheses to failure without even testing them, undercutting the means to make consciously-informed choices.

This subconscious default, I believe, is one of the most potent weapons in Mind's egoic repertoire. For by planting a negative bias as the basis from which we meet the unknown, the ego instinctively protects itself and its territory from the unwelcome intrusion of new ideas, ways of seeing and being. Evolution's inexorable pressure to move beyond existing eggshells, patterns and paradigms, however, continues to push the evolutionary envelope despite our inertial resistances; working like the attrition of water on rock, wearing it/us down grain by grain, drop by drop, doubt by doubt, until the dam finally gives way and we release in a flood, admitting, despite centuries of adamantly pragmatic ignorance, that the earth, after all, *is* round, that we *do* somehow revolve around the sun, that this seemingly-stable text *is* in fact composed of sub-atomic worlds spinning at such speeds that they appear motionless.

Once we consciously recognize this unconscious default pattern, then, following the trail of its kneejerk "No" back through evolution's compost heap of previously impossible notions, we can begin to identify and neutralize its influence in the present; freeing ourselves to consider and explore without bias or preprogramming such emerging possibilities as: Energy, light and matter are simply different forms, wavelengths and states of Consciousness; matter is the body of God; or the even-more-blasphemous proposition that money, once a utilitarian and facilitative device, has devolved into a powerfully-addictive, all-consuming habit and opiate of the ego that future species and their corresponding economies will eventually outgrow.

Applying this awareness to the work at hand as this Agenda gears itself down from premises to action-plans and proposals—to not only choosing as a species to mutate but consciously taking the steps to make it real, effectuating a choice that alters more than 13 billion years of subconscious evolutionary patterning—we should anticipate Mind's reactionary protest. For it is effectively being bypassed as the last word, final arbiter and reality-filter for Truth. It is only natural, then, that Mind, programmed by its egoic survival instinct, will use all of its resources to defend its morphogenetically-conditioned patterns, planting its generic thoughts and doubts in what we call "our" minds; which in turn assume these thoughts and doubts to be "ours," blanking out the fact that "our" minds/thoughts are simply the individuated forms and fractals, receivers and transmitters, for an archetypal mental principle of being: A macro-mentality, this Agenda contends, increasingly stressed and threatened by the emergence of an infinitely greater supramental principle.

In which case, it is not surprising that, motivated by Mind's defensive posture, we still find ourselves instinctively demanding proof that such a next evolutionary principle in fact exists before we will willingly accede to explore its reality. If we scratch beneath the surface of the demand, however, rather than getting trapped in its circular reasoning, we expose another contradiction. For the proof Mind is actually seeking is *mental* proof: proof in terms which the Mind *as it is* can comprehend, assimilate and certify via its mental instruments. But since this certification relies upon Mind's existing databank as a reference point—an egoic databank, however voluminous, limited to previously-acquired experiences, definitions and associations—there is no way to corroborate (or deny) dimensions beyond its threshold range. (Witness our mind-based science fiction attempts to project the future which, for the most part, portray both terrestrial and extraterrestrial characters as little more than high-tech versions of ourselves and our present conflicted level of consciousness, virtually dismissing the thematic concept of an evolution of consciousness.)

Such an apparently-reasonable demand, then, for evidence and reassurance before approving, let alone undertaking the unprecedented metamorphic exercise our choice implies, is existentially irrational, analogous to monkeys asking humans to verify and explain human consciousness in monkey terms. For the only way a monkey can understand human consciousness is *to become human.*

Just as the only way we can actually affirm the existence of trans-human beingness is to become it, becoming our own guinea pig in a radical evolutionary research where knowledge is lived, not borrowed or owned.

With this understanding, then, let us proceed to explore—which in terms of this applied research denotes a simultaneous will to experience—the directions and responsibilities that our our evolutionary choice implies; attempting to consciously cultivate, incarnate and implement the post-egoic qualities, values, orientations and survival strategies of an authentic trans-humanity; defining and distinguishing ourselves as we go, outgrowing the gravity of *egoicus*, lending ourselves to the momentum of *transitionalis*.

Moving from *Homo Egoicus* to *Homo Transitionalis*

The first quality, it would seem, essential in differentiating *transitionalis* from *egoicus* is simply the will to want to change. For all else unfolds from this will and intention. But for this will-to-change to be effective, it must be real, that is, motivated by a felt need and sense of urgency that our present state as a species is unbearable and unsustainable. Anything less, however idealistic or wishful, will fail or fall back into some intermediate comfort zone, unable to generate the breakthrough force and commitment to see us through the transition. In other words, if we are still divided in our will—if something in us is still not really convinced that we are facing our own extinction, does not sufficiently feel that to go on living as we are, individually and civilizationally, is suffocating—then egoic gravity will prevail, sinking us through that "leak."

This is as it should be. Because from an evolutionary perspective, we cannot fake or force change. In the case of *conscious* mutation, then, genuine pattern-shifts can only happen when the evolute finally recognizes that it must change to survive. And if that survival is predicated on the material association of ego with death—in other words, if we finally make the direct connection not only between ego-consciousness and inner suffering but with our accelerating outer frictions, disintegration and potential extinction—we raise the stakes and motivation for species-level change from morality to mortality; devising a new survival strategy accordingly, lending ourselves willingly to collaborate in our own post-egoification regardless of risk or sacrifice.

This transformational will-to-change distinguishes itself from our more ordinary uses and conceptions of will in that it implies a will to change everything, including the way we use our will. In which case, it is a willingness to both exercise *and* surrender one's will at the same time, in the same movement; acknowledging the need to change, activating a will toward the realization of that goal while relinquishing egoic control over results, expectations and timelines for the very evolutionary changes we seek; calling in a greater consciousness to oversee that change; turning over our caterpillar lives and selves to wiser, more compassionate and trustworthy hands. For caterpillars, no matter how super-caterpillified, can never through their own devices become butterflies. In fact, it is only the secret call of the butterfly within each larval being that leads us to the chrysalis. For why else would any creature willingly undergo the passage through its own metamorphic death were it not for the call to flight of a greater life within it?

To consciously collaborate with this new will and application of will, then, we must want, i.e., *will*, the evolutionary truth *whatever it may be*. In other words, it is not sufficient simply to want to change. We must want to change the very consciousness which wills that change, reminding ourselves, as Einstein put it, that we cannot solve problems through the same consciousness that created them. We must take great care, then, in this evolutionary "transfer of power" that, in our ignorance and blindness, we do not turn that metamorphic power back over to the same ego under a new name, allowing it to reinfect the very will-to-change with its hidden agenda, projected goals and problem-solving techniques.

For as an apprentice transitional species entering its phase-one "pupa" stage—that most vulnerable in-between stage where we can no longer rely on the past, on the security of what we have been and the egoic laws that governed us, yet we are still disoriented, ungrounded in what we are becoming—we need some trustworthy inner compass and guidance to safeguard us through the passage, protecting us from our own residual ego's corruptive Midas touch. In which case, it would seem, we must consciously discover or develop the essential psychological and intuitive equivalents that Nature encoded at the pre-conscious level through instinctive process in earlier life-forms undergoing metamorphosis.

I believe this inner compass, capable of seeing us through the flux of our confusions, fears and self-deceptions, already lies within us, its bearings set to and from our own true center. In fact, like the divine butterfly overseeing its own metamorphosis from within the caterpillar itself, it is, I believe, our own innermost psychic self who equips us with a first core sense that resonates like a tuning fork with what really rings true; providing us (providing we silence our restless minds and the cross-current of pulls and desires which obscure it) a torch to guide us through our blindness: A torch kindled from the innately self-luminous soul qualities of humility, sincerity and integrity; gradually shedding more and more light, growing stronger as we stoke it with our aspiration, opening us to greater clarity and transparence, silencing the frenzy of doubts and fears flittering like bats in our subconscious caves.

And in that gathering silence, that listening glistening silence that begins to fill our cocoon, we progressively open a transparent field and channel of communication with our true self; retraining our interim selves in that silence to a language that does not speak in words but in feelings and vibrations that resonate with the simple and true; clarifying and sifting out the egoic complications and counterfeits from the authentically inspired, pointing out the true directions and indications according to the degree of our sincerity, egolessness and self-giving.

It is in this sense, then, that I believe the first signs of a next species will not present themselves through showiness, glamour or exotic displays of power, but rather through humble, simple yet refreshingly real gestures: focused more on anonymous vibrational change rather than showcasing the appearance of or taking the credit for such change; uncompromisingly honest with oneself and, as a consequence, with others, while at the same time, extending oneself selflessly with others, remaining accessible rather than aloof, compassionately identifying with each one in their own way, speaking to each one in their own language, in a way that affirms their equality and validity, cutting through the self-glorifying spiritual double-talk to the common language and common sense of the heart, reminding us of things we have known all along but have simply forgotten, reminding us of the love that really matters despite the more charismatically-clever scripts, punditry and pseudo-knowledge which still enamor our minds.

If we wish to embark on this evolutionary journey, then, consciously setting sail from *egoicus* to *transitionalis*, we begin that voyage by

- willing that change;
- wanting the truth *whatever it may be* rather than blindly wanting what our ego still covets and, consequently, manipulating the "truth" accordingly to suit its predetermined ends;
- surrendering our will to an inherent evolutionary Wisdom that alone knows what we truly need, the methods to realize those true needs and the reality-timeline to get there, informing and enlightening us along the way so that we can begin to co-creatively collaborate, learning what it is we

need to learn and unlearn, know and unknow, ask and unask;

- developing the psyche-centric qualities of humility, sincerity and integrity, progressively aligning and integrating our multiple planes, sub-personas and behavior patterns around a more transparent post-egoic center as we transition forward and inward.

From such an inner groundedness, then, I believe we establish a trustworthy foundation upon which to build our plans, policies and actions, personal and collective. For by beginning from inner change and working outward—developing more sensitive and sensible inner instruments, means of perception and communication from which to initiate our work in the world, matching each outward step with an inner one, approaching our mutation from *egoicus* to *transitionalis* through the perspective of the evolutionary venture that it actually is—we build in the basis for a truly integral and sustainable sustainability.

Toward a More Integral, Trans-Human Sustainability

Through this more integrated and inclusive approach toward our evolutionary goals and unfolding futures, linking the effectiveness of outer change to an expanding inner consciousness, I believe *transitionalis* initiates us into a far more radical, relevant and egalitarian mysticism: A terrestrial, secular and material mysticism that demonstrates its wisdom and power by healing and changing not only the worlds within us, but translating that change progressively into the larger collective and planetary bodies we inhabit; moving us as a species from a transcendence-based spirituality to a transformation-based reality; recentering us in the post-egoic premise that we exist in one unbroken continuum of body-consciousness, not just body-mind.

With this new, terrestrial-oriented mysticism, then, which measures its evolution and efficacy by a far humbler yardstick, practice and "work ethic," we begin to redefine a more holistically-sustainable concept of sustainability itself; recognizing that we cannot establish the outer sustainability we seek without the counterpart inner sustainability to truly sustain it. In other words, we must create in ourselves a more sustainable, viable and adaptive consciousness if we would hope to understand what real sustainability means and how to achieve it.

It is *transitionalis*, then, who begins to rescue sustainability from the split-vision grasp of *egoicus*, reconciling a top-heavy orientation that continues to look for outer answers exclusively through outer problem-solving techniques and technologies, missing the key point that neither our cleverness nor our technologies can *solve us*. In fact, it is this primary dependence upon our prima donna sophistries and technologies that intensifies the problems, disempowering and diverting us more and more away from the very thing we need to change: ourselves.

For only when *we* change will we know how to use our sciences and technologies rather than being used by them; only when *we* change—self-mastering our endless stream of cravings and desires as we blindly seek things, people or pleasures to fill a hole in us which only our missing wholeness can fill—will we begin to become a truly sustainable (synonymous in this scenario with post-egoic) species; reversing the equation of consciousness from slavery to our unconscious habits and desire-mechanisms to consciously prioritizing and responding to genuine needs; creating in that reversal, value-based social and economic systems rather than mindlessly servicing the machinery of our quantity-based systems which continue to devalue and degrade us.

In which case, the very viability of our species and planetary ecosystem depends, I believe, on our willingness to practice and implement an inner sustainability—a sustainable *intra* as well as *inter*personal behavior, consciousness and lifestyle—*becoming*, as Gandhi said, the changes we wish to see in the world.

In other words, if we only focus on developing sustainable outer policies to respond to critical socio-environmental issues without paying equal attention to the evolution of a sustainable inner consciousness; if we only set our minds to brainstorming and legislating new socio-economic systems and reforms without changing the person who inhabits those new systems, we set ourselves up to repeat the failures of all revolutionary change, missing the critical missing link that distinguishes revolution from evolution, condemning ourselves to a half-way sustainability, which of course is a contradiction in terms.

This should not, however, become an excuse for inaction. For from the perspective of evolutionary triage, we must, ready-or-not, begin to address our most life-threatening, life-stressing symptoms *now*; reminding ourselves that we cannot wait at this critical evolutionary juncture for a more complete inner transformation to gracefully catch up with and overtake our outer crises, painlessly providing us with the perfect cure—which is why the prototypal transition of *transitionalis* is both the most perilous and most wrenching. For if we linger too long, politely waiting for just the right conditions, mass awareness and receptivity, it may be *too* late. *Egoicus*, after all, will not go willingly or cooperatively, at least not at the primary-shift stages where it still has wiggle room to rationalize and defend its hereditary patterning, denying the cliff toward which it is heading full-speed.

Operating from an evolutionary commonsense, then, we must mobilize ourselves to action even as we still struggle with our own inner gaps and blindspots; resolutely pursuing an evolutionary activism that courageously yet humbly begins from who and where we actually are; utilizing our will and resources however awkwardly to turn the earth-ship from its present geocidal course; doing the evolutionary "dirty work" to assure the physical and psychological survival/sustainability of ourselves and our planet *before* turning our attention to more sublime levels of metamorphic change; consciously accepting the thankless responsibility of the evolutionary warrior, the selflessly-heroic role of *transitionalis.*

For as the phase-one trans-species, *transitionalis* is the barrier-breaker who prepares the way, builds the sustainable ground, forgoing the more luminous inner unfoldings that remain for successive species; willingly and strategically sacrificing itself for the future self it is still to become; transforming the very concept of sacrifice from egoic loss to consensual (and eventually joyful) self-giving; transferring the very concept of self to an ongoing rather than fixed state of being; expanding our understanding of ourselves to an evolutionary scale and process where we become the very thing, the very consciousness, to which we give ourselves; paradoxically growing and enriching by our willingness to give, translating into material realities the meaning and myth of the Phoenix that rises triumphantly from its own ashes.

Repeating our premise in less mythic terms, sustainability is only sustainable in concept and practice if it incorporates inner as well as outer sustainability. Developing this more integral, trans-human interpretation of sustainability, then, let us continue to explore its implications, applications and challenges through contemporary examples and personal observations.

Coming from a background of intensive inner questing that prepared me more for a contemplative rather than life-confronting path, I found myself, beginning in the mid-1960s, drawn into a catalytic mix that merged my plunge into *yin* spiritual practices with a *yang* of protest movements, meeting processes, hands-on trainings, fieldwork applications and experiments focused on social and environmental change, community-building, personal/interpersonal healing and transformation. This "conspiratorial" process (which, in retrospect, I see as my dharma taking charge of my fate) pressed me from poetry and philosophy into personal and political activism, initiating me, often despite myself, into what I later recognized as the work of healing our formidable schism between inner and outer, spiritual and material. In other words, moving from transcending to transforming, in effect, expanding from single-issue activism, monocultural thinking and patrilineal mysticism to whole-spectrum evolutionary activism.

As I grew more consciously into my path, I left the States at the end of the 1960s and spent the next 21 years in the unique international community experiment of Auroville in south India. It was there in that microcosm and pressure-cooker of humanity (growing from a scattering of pioneers when I arrived to now more than 1,500 particpants from some 40 nationalities) that I began to learn from the ground up, under the most difficult circumstances and environments, what it means to actually lend oneself to a new life— what it means to front the devolutionary undertow in ourselves and the world if we would reach a truer shore.

This diverse range of inner-outer experience and intensive cross-cultural exposure became my ongoing teacher and guru, sometimes whispering sweet wisdoms in my ear, oftentimes informing me through crashing circumstances like a no-nonsense Zen master whacking me awake with a bamboo reality-stick. Nevertheless, this cumulative experiential field provided me with an invaluable first-hand database from which to observe and intuit personal and collective patterns, behavioral blindspots and disconnects, turning me among other things into something of an amateur anthropologist for a species-in-the-making.

One of my key "anthropological" discoveries in Auroville, consciously confirming in that collective process what I had already begun to vaguely sense or suspect through my 60s' initiations, was:

The quest for Light does not start from light or levity but rather places us precisely before everything that stands between us and the Light we seek; challenging us to confront, persevere and pass through our shadow, to run the gauntlet of all that opposes and resists within and around us—i.e., all that is still unconscious and, by virtue of that unconsciousness, is *pained by light,* preferring the egoic comfort of darkness and unseeing—if we would emerge into the clearing on the other side.

Since my return to the States in 1990, my subsequent ongoing learning, training and research, inner and outer, has continued to reinforce this premise that remains, I believe, at the core of our contradictory default programming, instinctively shying us away from the very light—or, for that matter, love, joy, freedom, truth, etc.— we call for, turning us back to shadier, more familiar patterns. (Which is why we half-jokingly admonish ourselves as a species to be careful what we ask for because we just might get it. Or why the priest, when pressed for transparence, instinctively pulls his frock that much tighter around him, revealing in that gesture of piety and propriety, the self-protective instinct of the spiritual ego and its preference for the façade of harmony rather than face the humbling contradictions that Truth dredges up.[1])

Illustrating this unconscious disconnect through collective example, it is not uncommon to witness in even the most progressive meetings and group processes the direct contradiction between professed goals and beliefs, and the actual behavior, interaction and communication in which the meeting vibrates. In other words,

---

1. Sri Aurobindo, in his incisive wit, noted this play between the religious reflex and the Divine's irreverent response through the following aphorism: "My lover took away my robe of sin and I let it fall, rejoicing; then he plucked at my robe of virtue, but I was ashamed and alarmed and prevented him. It was not till he wrested it from me by force that I saw how my soul had been hidden from me."

the same environmental or social activists (or their spiritual counterparts) who join together in common cause for planetary sustainability, peace and justice are not immune to infighting among themselves; confronting and acting out the very unresolved blockages within and between themselves they aspire to work out in the world; coming up against their own formidable egoic residue as they get down to the nitty-gritty realities of actually organizing, prioritizing or working out approaches and action-plans to achieve agreed-upon goals.

How many times in fact have we witnessed good meetings and good people with noble ideals and best-of-intentions fail miserably, disintegrating into the same egoic intolerances, abuses and disharmonies they point a finger at in their more institutionalized forms? This is because we still carry, despite our pro-evolutionary goals and rhetoric, that same unsustainable Trojan horse within each of us—that subtler, perhaps more benign or refined version of egoism that we see projected in its grosser corporate incarnations around us. So long as we do not acknowledge and simultaneously work to root it out within us, then, our meetings and community experiments will continue to carry forward the seeds of their own unsustainability, devolving back to our lowest conscious common denominator, succumbing to the gravity that distinguishes *re*volutionary from *e*volutionary change.

The solution to this problem, however, is not simply to throw up one's hands and go home from the meeting in frustration, defeated, disappointed and disillusioned by the process; nor is it to retreat into leave-me-alone monasticism; but rather to accept that the very frictions and blockages that present themselves are an integral part of what must be worked out and worked through if we are to forge a harmoniously-effective and *sustainable* will together—in other words, if we are to embody rather than merely promote the social, spiritual, ecological and economic changes we espouse. For to get from words to actions, we must be prepared to bear with the exposure of our egoic dirty laundry, not just pointing the finger smugly at the other but looking at one's own reflection in the mirror; tempering the merciless critic in us with the compassion of one who begins to see self in other, developing in the process the post-egoic communication skills, wills and perseverance to want the truth *whatever it may be*, whatever the egoic sacrifice; out-sustaining the intransigence of our shadows if we would liberate and empower our light. After all, we have nothing really to lose but our ego and the pain of its resistance; and in that loss, everything to gain.

If we want to truly evolutionize our meeting and decision-making processes, then, becoming a more effective force for sustainable change in the world, we must become inwardly viable and sustainable ourselves, modeling and practicing the same principles that we would apply to our institutions; recognizing that even the most ecologically-proactive among us is still conflicted (i.e., dis-ecological) within. It is far more challenging, after all, to apply ecology's integrally holistic nature to our own inter-species relationships than to the wildlife around us; far simpler to love a tree than a colleague, let alone a stranger armed with a chainsaw.

Though the application of this more integral sustainability highlights the need to bring outer actions and behaviors into alignment with inner goals and visions, the reverse is also true. In other words, we must take care not to fall into the opposite trap, over-emphasizing the need for inner sustainability and, in the process, creating the disconnect at the other end: i.e., turning exclusively toward inner change and a corresponding inner spirituality which effectively renders us materially impotent.

For by seeking out the very inner peace and poise we need to sustain us but unwittingly letting that peace become a goal and obsession in itself, drawing us farther and farther in until we lose our reality-balance, slipping, as noted earlier, into negation as solution, we relinquish the very holistic sustainability we seek; solving the problem of material existence by abandoning it; disenfranchising our relationship with earth's accelerating urgencies by buffering ourselves in a peace that simply numbs rather than heals us, effectively signing off on our personal and planetary bodies by declaring this reality an illusion.

But we cannot, as commonsense tells us, save half a reality, half an earth, half a person, choosing inner over outer or vice versa. Only a spirituality, then, that is itself sustainable—i.e., of an evolutionary and self-evolving nature, updating to incorporate emergent insights and expanding experience, willing to courageously face rather than flee a seemingly endless cycle of personal, cultural and collective shadows, contradictions and conflicts—can serve humanity in this terrestrial moment. Just as only an activism that simultaneously accepts to change not only *what* it sees but *the way it sees* can hope to resolve our inseparably-knotted global crises.

Diversity as the Evolutionary Path to Unity

The emergence of a new human species does not imply the supplanting or suppression of its predecessor species. Even in the relatively recent case of Neanderthals, for example, there was a period of transitional overlap when they coexisted for a period with their branching successor species who evolved into modern humans. In the case of a conscious mutation, however, as distinct from more genetically-subconscious mutational processes, this Agenda contends that the overlap would not simply follow historical evolutionary precedent: i.e., characterized by the successor species assuming the egoic role of the conqueror; replaying the dominator-dominated model and its interactive behavioral dynamic of competition, strife and, eventually, subjugation; leading in the case of the conquered either to extermination, enslavement or, at best, racial or class-segregated subservience.

In other words, more highly-evolved trans-humanities, this thesis suggests, will no longer operate from this archaic ego-reflex that sets emergent species into competition with their predecessors. For it is the mechanism of this primitive reflex—motivated by a genetic fear-based egoic coding that auto-labels that which is not "us" or "our kind" as threat, enemy, adversary, "them"—which, in turn, leads to an acting out of that reflex through personal, cultural, ideological or terrestrial turf wars for domination, control or consumption of resources; progressively expanding the definition of "them" while paranoiacally narrowing the definition of "us" into more and more restrictive clubs until our internecine clashes eventually turn us against everything, everyone, including ourselves.

As evolution, then, begins to break out of its own egoshell, moving from ego-centric to holo-centric unfolding, the relationship between ongoing human species and their predecessors will become more and more harmonious, symbiotic, creative and "syncreative," the more consciously-evolved lending their larger, more powerful consciousness to illumine rather than eliminate or lord over the less conscious; helping them come into their own light more gracefully through a process that co-equally shares realities; exerting a positive, embracing influence which dissolves the ego-inherited predatorial pattern that measures survivability in terms of destroying or dominating what it exceeds; replacing that pecking-order pattern with a more sustainable, collaborative and mutually-supportive inter-relationship: A new form of inter-species relationship that spontaneously springs from an expanded sense of self-identity, future humanities identifying with their predecessors as their own prior selves; and, as a consequence, humbly, compassionately, without condescension or judgment, identifying with the difficulties and challenges of their "younger siblings" as they struggle to emerge.

While the break-away movement of *transitionalis* from *egoicus* will certainly be marked, as we are already witnessing, by strife and friction as we struggle to disengage from the ego's death grip, habit-patterning and decision-making, I believe this is a temporal and transitional phenomenon that will diminish and recede as *transitionalis* continues to more consciously emerge. For as it gains a more conscious sense of itself and its emergence as a distinct interim species, finding its footing on a new ground and evolutionary basis of being, it will begin to implement a mutational shift in behavioral dynamic and relationship with *egoicus* as well as its own fellow "émigrés," setting a new momentum for future inter-species rapport. In fact, I believe, we are already witnessing the first translations of this shift through the advent of sensitivities and applied psychological researches such as conflict resolution, win-win paradigms, communication and listening skills, leading us toward more holistic and compassionate approaches to healing and harmonizing the differences that Ego Man dealt with by denying or destroying.

How can we consciously build upon this momentum, then, strengthening the emergent directions and practices through which *transitionalis* reverses the egoic gravity and polarity that programs us to equate other with enemy or competitor?—that confuses uniformity for unity and, consequently, triggers our primordial allergic reaction to diversity, priming our cellular and corporate selves to flee or conquer "others"?

The movement to embrace diversity in fact describes the physics of Love, expanding us beyond the ego's constrictive force-field into an ever-widening space, breath and sense of self until there is no other—until we have broken through to a Universe that not only centers around but *is* OneSelf, indivisible, whole, yet infinitely-diverse in its creative Self-expression and Self-experience. As this Evolutionary Agenda, however, has established in principle, we do not leap from this to That—in this case, from egoic otherness to OneSelf—in a single spiritual bound but rather through a series of graduated stages and metamorphic synapses in an exponential progression of consciousness.

In this progression, then, it is *transitionalis* who, at the species level, begins to trail-blaze our evolutionary path through ourselves to ourselves, consciously acknowledging in the process that *each of us is a world and path in ourselves*. In other words, each of us, despite outward similarities, shared generic characteristics and tendencies, is an unclonable combination of experiences, orientations, conditionings, levels of consciousness, degrees of integration, angles of perception, skills, speeds, challenges, capacities, potentials and destinies. Each of us has our own distinct signature, vibrational frequency, instrumentation and method of transcribing the larger evolutionary sheet music from which all of us consciously or unconsciously are playing; giving that music a personal touch, tempo, style and interpretation.

It would be a grave mistake, then, to impose our rendition on someone else, or to attempt to play someone else's version,[2] regardless of how impressive or attractive; just as it would be a torment to keep replaying one's own piece ad nauseam without some new inspiration to spiral it into another octave, reweaving and reintegrating common themes, threads, melodies and refrains into a new harmonic. Because in effect, these attempts to mimic or copy others, whether by choice or force, simply block and retard one's ac-

---

2. Rewording this proviso in a paraphrase from the *Bhagavad Gita*: It is better to follow one's own self-law (in Sanskrit, *sva-dharma*), however humble, than to assume that of another, however great.

tual process to become oneself. Just as the broken-record repetition of melodies and patterns we have already mastered ourselves keeps us locked within our own *intra*personal past, preventing us access to the flow of our future selves.

Through these metaphors, we remind ourselves to check that egoic tendency which crystallizes evolving truths into fixed dogmas, religions, laws; superimposing one-size-fits-all formulas or directives upon the sacredness of each person and moment; killing in the process the very life that keeps truths true; imprisoning ourselves and one another in ever-narrowing past forms of truth, personal or collective; worshipping Truth's icon and stamping it out in the ego's rigid die, then mass-marketing it to ourselves in a packaged uniformity from which the creative unity that once inhabited it has long since fled.

Cutting through the fog, confusion and disconnection between principles and practice, it is helpful, I believe, to illustrate how the uniform application or imposition of a generic truth—no matter how well-intended, how true in the abstract, how successful for someone else or for another time—may actually create the very obstacle to achieving the goal which that truth aspires to realize. For example, for those whose natures are more archetypically gifted or inclined toward work and service, i.e., toward the path which yogic traditions describe as *karma yoga*, it may well be counterproductive to begin one's conscious quest from a purely inner or meditative approach, assuming, as so many of us do, that the path to Truth runs essentially if not exclusively through meditation, book-learning and contemplative disciplines. In fact, such a "prerequisite"—based on artificial hierarchies and predetermined attitudes about what Spirituality is and isn't—may actually intimidate, discourage or undermine us from beginning our own true quest; confusing and turning us against our true natures, preventing us through that subversion from finding the door to our core self, which, after all, is the real entry-point to our life's quest.

The critical learning, then, in this process to find our true selves is to humbly identify who and where we *actually* are, letting that, and not some abstract spiritual notion, become the most direct means to get us where we need to go. In other words, designing the path to meet the nature rather than the other way round. In which case, our first work is to consciously recognize our own authentic self-nature, *sva-dharma*; our second, to accept it without judgment, without measuring it through our ego's ambitions or other people's mirrors, media and values; our third, to follow rather than deny it for some arbitrary path or discipline which one's mind or some influential guru-figure misguidedly insists must be our chosen path; having the courage to heed one's own sense of truth and, in so doing, honoring the uniqueness, equality and validity of all our pathways as we stumble and grope our way from darkness to light, recognizing that in this evolutionary journey, *all* roads lead us Home: All sincere seeking takes us where we need to go, bringing us to the person, the book, the insight, the moment where we need to be, placing us not only before the breakthrough we seek but all that resists that breakthrough.

Be suspicious, then, of teachings or teachers, regardless of how luminous or inspiring, that impose rather than adapt, setting up rigid hierarchies that demand conformity. For that is not, this thesis suggests, how the Divine operates. One should not, however, interpret this as a "release clause" from the intense disciplines, challenges and sincerity-of-purpose which this transformation asks of us. It is simply intended to remind us that we accept them freely as *self*-disciplines rather than as the overlay of others who would, regardless of good intentions, turn us into clones of *their* experience, path and perception.

Above all, then, we must summon the will to stay true to one's self, learning to distinguish its uniqueness from the flashy egoic forgeries others would sell us or we would sell ourselves; recognizing that while the Fire that kindles all evolution is one, it flames through infinite forms, colors and intensities. For the intellectually-oriented, then, this Fire flares through a more mental quest and hunger to know, translating in traditional yogic terms as the path of the *jnana yogin*. For the emotional and feeling-oriented, it expresses more spontaneously through the relational or devotional experience of the *bhakti yogin*. For the more active, outer-oriented, it communicates more naturally through hands rather than head, marking the archetype of the *karma yogin* whose work, craftsmanship and selfless service become the path to the Divine.

All of these diverse orientations, however, only differ in outer form, *not inner value*. The tree-planter or potter, then, sincerely following their natural paths, will get *there* just as effectively as the meditator, the visionary or the pundit; just as surely as the saint surrendered to her ecstasy. For in the Divine's Reality, we *are* all one, all equal, all equally valid and valuable, despite the egoic value systems, spiritual or secular, we unconsciously project upon ourselves and one another.

In any case, if the whole point of this evolutionary exercise is to get to the Whole Point, then we are not here just to perfect a predominant aspect or part of our nature but to fulfill our integral potentials and possibilities; rounding ourselves out; outgrowing the limits of our initial templates; becoming more than just a type—more than just thinkers or doers, empaths or lovers—as we move toward whole person-hood and a more holistic humanity; reuniting what translates through ego as oppositional and competitive forces into complementary energies and a more progressively conscious inter-personal and inter-species collaboration.

Understanding with the Body

One of the simplest yet most profound things I learned in Auroville was that physically working together with others toward a common goal, while lacking the apparent charisma and mystique of more esoteric disciplines and practices, was one of the healthiest and most efficacious ways to individually and collectively realize the Divine in Matter. For in the process, we simultaneously work through inner issues, obstacles and misunderstandings, healing our differences through a more direct method which bypasses mind and goes straight to the body as a way to harmonize, synthesize and divinize diversity in material forms and processes.

In other words, by moving from head-stuff to body-stuff—from meditation, cogitation or discussion in the abstract to an active meditation in Matter—we can actually resolve divisions within and between us that mere talk or psychological processing alone can't reach or address. In fact, in some cases, the talk and processing actually contributes to further complications. There is, after all, something extraordinarily healing about de-mentalizing: that is, slipping from our minds into our bodies and letting our bodies find the natural cellular rhythms and harmonies that one can only find when one frees the body from the chatter, dictates and abstractness of Mind.

In this de-mentalized scenario, then, one turns what we call physical work into something more akin to dance; liberating our bodies into vessels for a simple, joyful, creative harmony that, I believe, *is* the natural state of being; allowing ourselves to thaw from our mental rigidities and melt into our truer rhythms together. In fact, I can still vividly recall through body-remembered imagery such an experience that in many ways defined for me the pioneering Auroville spirit of the 1970s. It takes the form of a hundred hands passing pans of concrete for hours along a human thread at a construction site; feeling the heavily-laden pan move lightly, effortlessly, weightlessly from one set of hands to the next . . . from

151

mine to hers to his, from dark-skinned to light, Westerner to Asian, villager to cosmopolitan, elder to youth, rich to poor . . .

. . . Weaving us all concretely together; building the builders as well as what we built; simplifying and synthesizing us all into one diversely-creative body in motion as we worked literally through the night to the following dawn; resolving through that body-process all the blockages we brought with us; clearing out the frictions to which our minds still clung; finding ourselves somehow spontaneously smiling at the person next to us who turns out to be precisely the one we couldn't stand yesterday; feeling ourselves unburdened of our divisions and discords as the flow of a living harmony overtook us all, releasing us from the conflicts that no longer made sense, letting them flush through that flow, dissolving like things of no substance back into the nothingness we waste our lives fighting over.

And that next morning, as the sun rose following what should have been a totally exhausting night, I actually felt stronger, gaining a strength and stamina that did not belong to me: A strength and joy that the body can only know from giving itself to something larger; and in that process, becoming a channel for an inexhaustible Force of Being, tapping in at some humble, personal level to the very secret that sustains this universe in a flow of Divine Love: a Force of Love that forever grows by self-giving.

Through this rediscovery of collaborative physical work, then, as an alchemical rather than merely mechanical process, elevating it from drudgery to dance, I began to understand how this next evolutionary power and principle could actually work more effectively, directly and sustainably through our bodies than through the often-distorting and complicating machinery of our minds; transforming the world around us by the lever of an inner will and willingness to simply *do* what needs to be done. For through this simple yet decisive call-our-own-bluff action, stepping out of the mind-field of doubts and impossibilities to *just do it*, a growing handful of Aurovillians proved Margaret Mead's axiom "that a small group of thoughtful, committed citizens can change the world."

For not only did we construct our homes, schools, communities, farms and collective infrastructure from scratch on a barren plateau in the middle of nowhere; but, over a period of two decades, this motley crew of human mutineers reforested over two million trees, transforming a severely-eroded and degraded landscape back into lush multi-species tropical forests; bringing back wildlife that hadn't been seen in the region for half a century; in effect, reversing the devolutionary gravity of death to birth new life; demonstrating what can be done by the power of simply *doing* rather than *thinking* it; preparing in that humble gesture the ground for the emergence of a viable, progressive community: A community that, despite its ongoing contradictions and denial systems, points us toward that community of humanity we must all grow into, levered by our accelerating crises toward a new species which no longer takes its cues exclusively from Mind: A trans-humanity which begins to understand with and through the body.[3]

---

3. In the late 1960s, it was through Mirra Alfassa (whom I knew simply as the Mother of the Sri Aurobindo Ashram) that I first heard the phrase "understand with the body." As Sri Aurobindo's co-partner in their unique evolutionary undertaking, she understood the imperative need to em*body* vision; aspiring and actually attempting through her 95 years to heal our spiritual-material schism; working not only toward inner liberations and realizations but toward a metamorphic transformation reflected at the cellular level. For she willingly made a laboratory of her own body, in effect, not only silencing her mind and surrendering egoic control, but consciously invoking a next supramental consciousness to enter through that transparence and begin acting directly upon the body and its organic functioning.

It is in this sense that I believe we must begin to shift our twenty-first century vision and decision-making from cerebral to body-based; cutting through our debilitating mental be-wilderness that immobilizes us as a species, so easily talking or scaring us out of the obvious things we urgently need to do; feeding us an endless stream of cautions, diversions and digressions, spiritual or secular, to maintain the egoic dominion of Mind. For what this radical notion of physical work is actually suggesting is nothing less than the overthrow of that authority; proposing that our next stage of evolution, by virtue of its *supra*mental nature, will bypass the distorting intermediaries of an egoic mentality to begin acting directly upon the simplicity and transparence of the body, humbling Mind from a decisionmaker and authority figure to an administrative instrument at the service of a truer wisdom and power.

What good is it, after all, to aspire for a new Reality, a new Consciousness, if we continue, unintentionally or otherwise, to ignore or neglect the body we inhabit and share, passively or actively destroying her in the interim, failing to make the crucial connection in time between inner and outer? What good is it to mythologize about enlightenment under the bodhi tree while the forests are being cut done around us, ripped off as a commodity or sacrificed for grazing lands to feed our fast-food habits?

These questions are all-the-more imperative for those of us who already see the writing on the evolutionary wall, who have caught the gist of a new genetic and trans-human script. For with this new sense comes new responsibility. We must take great care, then, to see that this new knowledge does not get usurped by the personal ego, twisted to private ends which would claim the incoming evolutionary Power for our small selves; in effect, withdrawing like some master sorcerer into his tower to wrest from the Divine a personally-transformed body or occult control over Matter while our terrestrial organism and its life-systems still succumb to the macro-ego's blindness, disconnection and greed.

For we are, like it or not, know it or not, one body. And the pain of our shared collective body—of the women savaged in Afghanistan; the rainforests torched in Brazil; the massacre of wildlife for trophies, trinkets or aphrodisiacs; the peasant covered in pesticides off-loaded wholesale to third worlders from our own banned arsenals of first world toxins; the homeless stick-figures wandering in a Rwandan desert or a New York subway—will continue to invade us through our dreams and dreads, through our semi-permeable membranes and natures; reminding us in undeniable experiential terms of the contradiction our egoic minds refuse to see; reminding us through the more direct exchange of feelings and sensations that, no matter how much we try to insulate or cut ourselves off from the pain and the life around us, we remain cellularly interconnected in one inseparable continuum of Being.

That terrestrial pain, then, will continue to slip through our defenses and denials, resonating as a background tension, angst and anguish from which we cannot escape until we have understood and confronted the responsibility of our Oneness: Until we have accepted to heal the pain together. For it is not only "your" pain or "mine" that we exclusively feel, but *all* of our collective inter-species suffering. All of the pain our un-oneness inflicts upon us.

If we would heal that pain, then, that shared collective well of pain, we must begin to pay attention to our bodies, feeling what we *actually* feel rather than what we *think* we feel or should feel, reorienting ourselves in the process to act from that more direct body-consciousness. It is the body, after all, that lets us know precisely who and where we are. For unlike the egoic mind, conditioned to lie and manipulate truth to justify its desires or denials, the cellular body at its core is simply a transparent instrument which reflects the consciousness that inhabits it. In this sense, the body has no agendas or ulterior motives other than to be.

If the body is sick, then, or weak and fatigued, it is not because of something the body has done wrong but because of some unconsciousness or distortion we—"we," meaning here our mental wills, egoic cravings and subconscious habit-patterns—have imposed upon it, effectively subverting the body-consciousness from its natural state and instincts. For example, if we smoke or indulge in other self-destructive habits, the body simply, impartially and amorally mirrors the results. It is not the body, however, that initiates such addictions, as we can attest from personal childhood experiences. For how many of us can honestly say that when we puffed a cigarette for the first time or curiously sipped dad's scotch, we liked it? Using our childhood bodies (and their essential innocence prior to subsequent *adult*eration) as a litmus test, then, we can see how we have forced and negatively conditioned our bodies to deny their own experience, imposing our ignorance and ignorant habits upon the body until it finally stopped protesting and gave way, accepting the violation as normative behavior, losing its innate sense of cellular discrimination as it succumbed and eventually became addicted to the perversion of patterns imposed upon it.

The result, however, despite our denial systems, deceits, self-excuse mechanisms and rationalizations, is that the body, personal or planetary, still *literally* translates the effects of this imposed unconsciousness through illnesses, dysfunctions, depressions and eventually death. If we are to succeed, then, in our evolutionary task, we must begin, both as a species and as individuals, to reverse this imbalance, learning to re-listen to and understand once again with our bodies; applying ourselves like a mother protecting her child. For the body, in this sense, *is* our child and the off-spring of our consciousness. In which case, we must develop the sense and sensitivities to heed its body-language, attending to its guileless cellular messages in the same way that we would respond to the pre-verbal gestures through which an infant communicates its needs to us.

Transposing this cellular principle from personal application to macro-policymaking, we must reverse our present species-level reference point for the way we prioritize and implement decisions. In other words, an evolutionized humanity will effectively take its cues *from* the earth-body rather than laying its arbitrary demands *onto* her; letting her transparently tell us her true needs, thresholds and tolerances rather than blindly imposing our ignorant minds, desire-driven wills and insatiable appetites upon her, in effect, as we are witnessing through *egoicus*, ripping her off and subconsciously manipulating the evidence to justify our actions or deflect our guilty conscience, avoiding the fact that through this denial we place ourselves and our entire terrestrial web of life at risk.

A maturing trans-humanity, then, will sensitize itself to read earth's trustworthy body-signs and signals, designing human policies, strategies and plans accordingly. In which case, it is the role of *transitionalis* not only to understand but to put into practice the direct link between staying true to ourselves and staying true to our bodies; learning to trust them, letting our cellular and terrestrial body-awareness become our trans- and post-mental teachers, guides and policymakers; learning through that emerging consciousness-in-matter to locate *exactly* what we need, *exactly* what we must do, *exactly* what we must change; cutting through our endless egoic denials to identify the actual points of resistance in ourselves and our cultures in order to consciously release them, outgrowing our pain as we learn to embrace our joy.

It doesn't take a Ph.D., after all, to recognize the omen of melting icecaps or holes in the ozone layer, connecting the dots between the pollution and progressive toxification of our biosphere and the out-of-control greed and ignorance which chairs our global economies. No more than a child needs a complex formula to connect the smell of a rose with a smile.

EIGHT

TOWARDS A POST-MONETARY SOCIETY[1]

Transformation at the personal and collective level is an integral action and undertaking that incorporates every aspect of our lives. For the sake of this Evolutionary Agenda, however, if I were to single out one key element, one root terrestrial power and bastion of resistance that needs to be held up to the mirror, brought into focus and stared down, it would be money. For in practical evolutionary terms, I believe that money—and the extraordinary power we have given it—represents in this moment of earth-time the most potent means and mechanism to keep us stuck, distorting our values and priorities, confusing us from seeing clearly and simply what we can and must do as a species; in effect, becoming the egoic carrot as well as the stick to keep us imprisoned in fear-based patterns and determinisms, black-mailing us to insure our allegiance and loyalty, convincing us before we even begin an inquiry into its nature and origins of the impossibility to function without it.

---

1. This chapter was originally drafted in 1997, long before beginning the manuscript of this book. It incubated in a drawer until it was finally published in article-format in the August, 2000 edition of *The Sentient Times*, a Northwest regional journal focused on "Alternatives for Personal and Community Transformation." It ironically appeared at the crescendo of Wall Street's heydays, when the Market was at its zenith, the culture was awash in cash, and money-mavens, like pied pipers, were leading us toward the promised land of endless prosperity.

In this context, I believe one of our key millennial and species-level goals is to reorient ourselves toward a post-monetary society and civilization. To achieve this formidable goal, however, (which for *egoicus* is blasphemous even to suggest, setting us against the cultural current that has systematically defined and dictated our societal values and historical directions for centuries) is not something we can realistically hope to achieve in some all-at-once leap to a utopian society. For as this thesis has developed in previous chapters, such myopic thinking sets us up to fail, ignoring the fact that evolutionary change is metamorphic and marathonic in nature rather than some one-shot, magic-mantra affair.

In other words, there are no spiritual short-cuts to circumvent evolution. The shortest and most direct path, then, begins when we stop our egoic attempts to skip steps; humbly accepting to begin at the beginning, at the front door; willing to go through whatever it takes to get us where we need to go; which in evolutionary terms means penetrating through the very mass and intransigence of the pattern we seek to change. If, as earlier chapters have pointed out, a pattern's mass is psychologically measured in terms of pattern duration multiplied by number of followers, then a pattern's resistance to change is relative to how long it has been repeated and how much weight (i.e., followers) it carries, shorter patterns with smaller numbers of repeaters presenting less mass than older, heavier habits with millions or billions of devotees and true believers.

To move from a money-based to a post-monetary economy, then, one must pass through the formidable gravitational "shadow" that pattern casts, penetrating through its devolutionary vortex of doubts and oppositions designed at every level to preserve status quo realities and egoic control. In which case, to run the gauntlet of the prevailing pattern and its cumulative nega-gravity, we must gear ourselves down, working at first through humble, incremental shifts and changes as we gradually build momentum toward more critical-mass breakthroughs and metamorphic synapses.

For it is only through a persevering evolutionary will that we can hope to manifest such radically new personal and societal patterns, norms and institutions, consciousness determining form rather than the other way round.

In the case of metamorphosing to (i.e., growing into) a post-monetary consciousness and its corresponding post-monetary society, then, we must be willing to go through the shadow of all that denies it, all that convinces us of its impossibility. From the perspective of this Evolutionary Agenda, such an attempt begins by

- dispelling the myth that money is simply the practical and facilitative device it once was;
- establishing, despite preconditioned denial mechanisms, that we are in fact mesmerized, addicted to and controlled by the egoic force behind money, possessed by our possessions through that tight-fisted force and its insatiably compulsive need to possess more.

For only then, motivated by the conscious recognition of this addiction, can we

- find the leverage and conviction to free ourselves from money's distorting codependency and the destructive behavior patterns, pseudo-priorities and values it generates; and
- redirect our personal and species-level will toward the practical manifestation of a post-monetary reality, healing ourselves from the daily conflict and contradictions which a "Monetocracy" has created in our lives.

To achieve this goal, we must graduate our approach, putting our evolutionized sense of time and timing into practice; breaking down a venture of such evolutionary scale and proportion into successive steps, stages and species-level agendas; recognizing that we cannot expect to realize through an emergent *transitionalis* the more complete changes and integral shifts that belong to a future holistic humanity far beyond what our present species-level visions and capacities can comprehend, assimilate or bring forth. In other words, we must avoid the trap that would default us at the outset to the ego's impatience and myopic timelines as a framework and reference point for this exercise, aware that we are beginning the evolutionary assault of the egoic Bastille, taking on the full force of the power that finances and sustains it.

The Mesmerism of Money

To rouse us from money's mesmerism, dispelling the myth of its immortality, we still require a hefty jolt of reality-shock therapy. For the sake of this exercise, then, let us construct a hypothetical scenario that amps up the voltage, providing an exaggerated contrast so that we can begin to see and feel for ourselves just how deeply we have bought into money—how insidiously invasive, addictive and controlling this intermediary has actually become in our lives. It is only the exaggeration, intensification and shock of pain, after all, that seems finally to get our attention, motivating us to reluctantly move forward from our this-is-the-way-it-is-and-always-will-be inertia.

Imagine, then, the following flash in tomorrow's news: *Bankruptcy of the dollar-world, collapse of federal monetary currencies as means of exchange and index of wealth.*

Living in a hyper-commercialized society immersed in money, such a scenario immediately conjures up images of mass hysteria: of a traumatized Wall Street and Main Street for whom these nightmarish heresies would pitch the world and order-as-we-know-it into chaos.

But, if we allow ourselves to step back from our initial panic-attack reactions to dispassionately question their auto-logic and ra-

tionale, what *are* such primal apprehensions, assumptions and reactions based upon? Is it just the obvious fear of out-of-control
breakdown? Or is that primary-level reflex itself just a smokescreen
to block us from actually pursuing the matter to a deeper level of
inquiry where, I believe, we will expose such default anxieties as the
ego's threshold-guardian response to stop us in our tracks from
calling the Emperor's bluff?

If we would actually *choose*, then, as a species to begin consciously making our own choices, exerting an authentic free will
rather than continuing to delude ourselves with its egoic forgeries
that merely repeat and defend status quo habit-patterns and call
that "choice" and "free will," then reevaluating money's sacrosanct
role in our collectively-shared reality is not only a legitimate but essential question: Is it still a valid currency for conducting the truer
transactions of our twenty-first century lives? Or is it merely something we have inherited and, through that subconscious inherit-
ance, mechanically perpetuate indefinitely, accepting its supremacy
and necessity without ever requestioning its real-time relevance and
impact? For if we can establish through common-sense inquiry that
money no longer serves our greater interest or that of our planet's,
that we in fact are serving it rather than it serving us, then I believe
it is our obligation and responsibility as a species to change things,
which in evolutionary street language means to do the right thing.

Let us take a good hard look, then, at our reaction to the theoretical crash of our dollar-driven economies; approaching the issue
not just as an economic phenomenon but as a psychological one.
For I believe that first terrified response to such a crash actually
reflects the corporate and societal-conditioned mentality/behavior
of substance abusers caught in the pathology of addiction,
codependency and denial—in the terror and trauma of withdrawal,
in this case, from the millennial habit of money, its systemic possession and the extreme power-high associated with it.

Perhaps the problem, then, is not really the radical proposition of moving from a monetary to post-monetary system but the speed at which we make the transition. For looked at from our future rather than our past, it is not really change which is the problem, but the abruptness, shock and consequent resistance to it, like the addict suddenly disconnected from his drug rather than weaned consciously and compassionately in more manageable steps and processes. Because for the addict trapped in the distortion of his drug, the terror of suddenly breaking free is the very mechanism that imprisons him and seals his doom. The first critical step, however, in personal or cultural recovery from an addiction is to admit that we have one.

If we allow ourselves, then, to get beyond that first primal shock to more gradually and methodically explore the deeper implications of a money-free economy, what in fact would really happen if somehow the dollar-sign coefficient was simply removed, unhooked from all our economic equations? What would we see, what would remain once we were "clean and sober"? Would we find that all was lost, Civilization reduced in some Mad Max scenario to a pile of rubble? Or would we find, once the dust had settled, that our *perception* of things had changed? That we saw the same landscape that had been there before, but differently, changed, because an enormous distortion had been removed, revealing in that transparence what is *really of value*?

Pursuing this inquiry, we need to remind ourselves that our civilizations and cultural constructs do not merely exist in the near-sighted span of historical time but in immeasurably larger cycles of evolutionary time—that despite our presumption as a species, we're still mere kindergartners whose raw hominid roots spiral back millions of years, our "civilized" heads hardly above water for 10,000 years or so in the oceanic billions it took to get to us. In this context, then, the advent of money is a temporal device, an historical adaptation that, if we honestly acknowledge its present cumulative "side-effects," may be outliving its evolutionary utility or, at the very least, primed for a creative mutation.

In this sense, let us deflate money to humbler human proportions, recovering in the process a simpler commonsense which uses the GOC (growth of consciousness) as its reference point for value and quality of life rather than the almighty GDP or the more recent market indices we have unwittingly allowed ourselves to worship. For by demythologizing the inflated power money has claimed in our lives, reminding ourselves that it was not always indispensable, that *we* created the dependency, I believe we create a level field to challenge its sovereignty.

The Origins and Evolution of Money

Our earliest pre-monetary economies evolved out of a more natural ecology that had no need for the artificial intermediaries of money or salary to motivate. The act of creation was still its own reward: One needed to eat, one discovered or devised the means; one needed shelter, one built it or bore with the elements.

As families, however, extended to clans and tribes, self-production likewise extended to incorporate the direct exchange—bartering—of work and goods cooperatively out of a common-sensed necessity and common-denominator survival. Eventually, as tribes widened or became nomadic, travel led to trade, exposing isolated communities to new goods, foods, crafts, tools and ideas. And with this diversification of trade (and thought) came not only the direct barter of goods and services but the introduction of objects to which we attributed aesthetic or shamanic value: rare shells, precious metals, beads and gems. Though still bearing intrinsic worth, this form of exchange represented a first step toward symbolic rather than direct value.

As trade and cross-pollination continued to grow with the increasing interaction and complexification of human societies, the need for more standardized "units of value" emerged, resulting in the minting of coins and eventually paper currency. Initially, the more universally accepted intermediaries of exchange were either coined from precious metals or were bank notes representing actual gold or silver equivalents held in reserve and redeemable on demand. This intervention marked the transition from pre-monetary to monetary-based societies.

In our present stage of monetary evolution, however, one would be truly hard pressed to find any such traces of intrinsic value or equivalents. Pennies are only copper-plated while dollars, Euros and yen have simply become accepted habits of exchange whose real value lies more in the trees cut down to print them rather than the glint of gold they replaced in some distant tribal memory. And now, even our paper currencies give way to the ever-more-abstract Pandora of plastic as we head toward a brave new world of cyber-banking and cyber-transactions where one's net worth is no longer contained in a bank vault but in the hard drive of a computer, virtually erasing all traces of human fingerprints, replacing binary-coded digits and a password-accessible sum for the tangible labor and heartfelt creations of four digits and an opposable thumb. Placing our trust in a strange God indeed.

How in fact did we get ourselves out on this limb?—this precarious point where needs and values are so skewed that our concept of net worth, like our currencies, becomes worthless, dehumanized and denatured, with no reference any longer to core inner values—to *who one is* rather than *what one has*—and as a consequence, that money is no longer simply a facilitative device, a means to something of *actual* value, but an end and value in itself: A distorting dead-end value. For if we can establish a direct link between money and the degradation of true net worth, revealing that money-measured and money-motivated values have in fact set us on a collision course with our own true selves, then we provide our species the critical information to adapt and evolve accordingly; priming us to embark on a transition far more perilous, profound yet rewarding than the ego-riddled progression from pre-monetary to cash-or-charge economies.

To pursue this line of inquiry, then, let us fast-forward a century or two, looking back on our late twentieth-century societies and their value systems, retracing the steps that brought us to this branch of the limb on which we're precariously dangling.

The Contradictions of Communism and Capitalism

Communism, with some stubborn exceptions, had just flat-lined from an overdose of bureaucracy, an arthritic apparatus and command structure whose droning lack of imagination stifled the infusion of new life and initiatives essential for a system's regeneration and health. Former communist states were selling out, buying into a capitalism which gloated in its apparent triumph. But did this finally portend the wholesale conversion to marketplace monotheism or was the capitalist cult prematurely celebrating what would turn out to be a pyrrhic victory?

With communism, the weaknesses as a competitive economic system were obvious: Lack of personal incentive and a pervasive sense of diminished individuality led in the Soviet scenario to lethargy, dependency and the eventual decline to a wheezing vodka-nomics unable to compete with the speed-junkie marketeers from Manhattan. Marxist-socialist principles and planning—state-run and regulated to ensure the fair value of labor and protect the working proletariat from oppressive owners who controlled the assets of production—inevitably led to top-heavy political systems and rigid hierarchies, the working masses trading off personal liberties for (apparent) job stability and basic economic security.

These well-intentioned welfare systems, however, as they marched lock-step toward their collectivist extremes, devolved into contradictions, replacing the tyranny of bourgeoisie owners with the tyranny of bureaucrats, abuse of power passing from private ownership to the state, degrading from Leninist ideals to ruthless Stalinist realities.

In the case of capitalism, the pathologies were more convoluted, masked in the rhetoric of individual freedom and free enterprise. Market economies originally evolved from legitimate supply-and-demand needs, goods and industries created to meet these needs in an apparently self-governing system. This free-market mechanism, however, could not foresee two coinciding events that would destabilize the equation: Populations began exploding at the same time that we started tampering with the needs themselves. In other words, capitalist enterprise began creating whole media industries to artificially fabricate and inflate needs in order to attract more buyers, effectively increasing demand and consumer ratio just as our population curve was taking off.

These new ad and marketing industries grew more and more disconnected from reality, obscuring the common *eco* roots of *ecol*ogy and *eco*nomics, mandated only to sell without taking into consideration the supply-side of the equation or the legitimacy of the needs. At which point the production and consumption of goods and services lost its balance, subverted from real needs and values to blind competitive principles ultimately driven only by profit or greed, sustainability be damned. It had not yet occurred to us as our populations rose exponentially that there was only so much we could *afford* to consume regardless of how much money we had.

As a result of this blindness, things began to exaggerate and distort: Franchise coffee houses competing on the same block with local beaneries because java was a hot commodity. Rival cereal-makers offering the same product in different artificial colors and flavors, the recipes prepared by ad-men rather than nutritionists as they vied for the child-market. A tobacco industry not only producing a product we know contributes to much of our healthcare costs but utilizing its scientists and lawyers to deny the while fighting for the right to finance seductive ads to assure itself a fresh supply of consumers to replace the ones it killed off. A federal Administration in the 1980s with such misplaced loyalties that it turned its considerable resources to vehemently deny global warming, the link between industrial/automobile emissions and greenhouse gases, acid rain or the depletion of our protective ozone layer.

How distorted could we get, prepared to commit ecocide rather than betray our corporate benefactors? Like communism in pursuit of its own extreme, capitalism *in extremis*, then, turned into an even more dangerous contradiction. For while marketplace economics appeared to align itself with democratic freedoms and the supremacy of the individual over the tyranny of the state, it unwittingly lent itself to the tyranny of the multinationals who in fact usurped the power and, in many respects, the role, of the state, in the end wielding that power and determinism of events no less ruthlessly than other dictatorships—the irony being that, as things came full circle, there was little difference between the corporate tyrants of capitalism and the bourgeoisie demons of communism. In fact, the very efficiency and infectiousness of capitalism would in many respects render it far more self-destructive than the more sluggish failures of communism.

The Karma of Carte Blanche Capitalism

Looking back at ourselves through this exercise, the absurdities become so much more transparent. How, we wonder as we rerun the tapes, could we have committed such blatant follies, rewarding entertainers and sports stars so disproportionately to the urgent and pressing needs of the time, standing by helplessly (or secretly admiring) clever investors and entrepreneurs who traded our future for short-term profits? False profits from dangerously false prophets.

What could we possibly have been thinking then? Or perhaps we will see what we simply couldn't admit at the time: That despite our veneer of reason, we weren't thinking at all. We were simply lost in the Nero-fiddling end-stages of post-industrial denial, escaping, medicating, anesthetizing ourselves any way we could from the overwhelming angst and responsibility of getting out of the mess we and our biosphere were in. And money—and the short-term fantasies it could buy us—was our drug.

How else to explain the insanity?—the illusions we fed ourselves in those late 1900s, when so many parents would barely get to even see their children grow up, lost in an absurd system where they had to neglect their kids in order to support them; when so many gifted and creative youth would never get to find their real gifts, contribute their real possibilities, experience the joy of their *true* net worth because their parents couldn't afford the education necessary to liberate those talents—those *true* values—or the time to nurture them.

How many uncounted miscarriages simply because we had lost all sense of value, purpose, priorities, hope? How many scientists, poets, planners and visionaries lost in the trade-off with money-making as we created an entire class of industries to numb or delude us of our hopelessness and despair?... Las Vegas clones springing up all over, even on tax-free Indian reservations as the colonized temporarily turned the tables on the colonizers; parasitic industries metastasizing like cancer cells with their get-rich-quick schemes and scam artists, telemarketing us, psychic networking us, even turning the New Age into just another marketplace where Dow merged with Tao and the indiscriminate seeker was fair game. A time, we would recollect one day, when nothing was sacred anymore. Nothing except the art of making money. By whatever means. Buy whatever means.

Competing Ourselves Out of Existence

The message, despite lip service to the contrary, that we actually sent ourselves in those parting twentieth-century moments was that cleverness, ruthlessness and manipulation pay; are role models to emulate and streetwise skills to cultivate. For while we indignantly decried violence, we conceded enormous power to the NRA and carnage-themed videogame-makers; while we proclaimed an end to the abuse of women, our ads, tabloids, internet and porno industries still capitalized on it. And paralleling our domestic hypocrisies, our blind-eye foreign policies accorded Most Favored Nation status to significant trade partners such as China despite flagrant human rights abuses and its death-hold takeover of Tibet (which, witness Kuwait, could never have happened if something like oil rather than mere human lives and culture were at stake). All because money somehow became our bottom-line decision-maker, usurping our (pretense of) free will, common sense and common decency.

In other words, what sells gets the last word. And for our conscience-free economies of that era, guns sold, exploitation sold, lying and violence sold. In fact, became acceptably if not fashionably addictable.

Looked at from our future, these schizophrenic behavior patterns, I believe, are the symptoms of a species caught in the vicious cycle of substance abuse; impulsively acting out of the moment with little concern for consequences; suffering from a severely impaired perception of reality and value that simply could not yet see (or chose to ignore) the connection between money, competition and violence: The connection between a system that defines success by defeating one's opponents and the toxic by-products generated by such a mercenary system: i.e., distrust, deceit, ruthlessness, insensitivity, paranoia, pollution as a cost-cutting measure at the expense of the environment, in effect, reducing Nature and neighbors to commodities subject to hostile takeover if the price is right.

An extremely risky phase that humanity in its ongoing evolution would have to pass through despite its denials and a cynicism that could not yet visualize a more successful, graceful and enlightened economics based upon primary values, equality, mutuality, voluntary simplicity and conscious collaboration. A cynicism still patronizingly dismissing such notions as wildly impractical utopian ideals. But despite the smugness of our conventional wisdom then, we would eventually be forced to ask ourselves as we strung ourselves further and further out on that limb, feeling it begin to crack beneath the weight, *what was the alternative?*

Reclaiming our True Net Worth

Returning, then, to present realities—to the branching point where we find ourselves now torn between two gravities, one drawing us down like a fist clenching, pulling us back through the familiar call of our egoic black hole, the other extending an open hand from our own future selves, inviting us forward into our adventure of consciousness—which do we choose? In other words, rephrasing the choice, are our existing money-driven economies viable paths to a sustainable future? Can we continue to abdicate responsibility, turning to Federal Reserve Board chairmen or market analysts to manipulate the answer? Or do we need a deeper wisdom and motivation to heal us of the havoc we have created in ourselves and our world?

These questions bring us to an unprecedented crossroads, facing us with a choice and series of choices that, I believe, will determine our survival or extinction as a species. For if we are unable to make critical evolutionary adaptations, if we stubbornly cling to our historical habits, addictions and mechanistic world-views, allowing the earth-ship to continue to drift, we may deceive ourselves for another few decades, tampering with or reinterpreting the mounting evidence. But eventually, that long rope evolution generously allows us runs out, tangled into a noose fashioned out of our own cleverness.

The transition to a post-monetary society begins as an inner journey, as a movement toward a post-monetary consciousness preceding the manifestation of its outer reality. Its critical phase-one shift begins, then, with the willingness simply to accept the possibility and commonsensibility of a such a concept, cutting though the prejudices that previously dismissed the notion as laughable, delusional or reckless. For by openly acknowledging the legitimacy and logic of such an economic goal, (we are not, after all, suggesting the elimination of economies, only the phasing out of the monopoly money we play with as if its real), in fact, by recognizing this goal as a target to lever us forward in an evolutionary progression to reclaim true net worth and value from the real madness that presently possesses our species, we prepare the conscious ground for its material emergence, inviting and calling the concept of post-monetary economics into the earth's noetic atmosphere as a first step to rooting it into material realities.

This inner journey, as with all hero journeys, then, begins with a willingness to sail off the edge, breaking free from the intimidating gravity of a flat-world mindset: A mindset that in this scenario reduces living systems to mechanics, crudely dissecting and disconnecting them in order to egoically know, own and control them. In which case, we are not only embarking upon an economic venture but a journey toward healing and wholeness, rounding the corners of ourselves and our planet, our ways of knowing, being and decisionmaking, widening in the process our definition of self as well as wealth...

...Redrafting our maps as we voyage into the uncharted territories of ourselves and what we can become; replacing the charts patterned by flat-world thinkers and economists who would reduce, for example, the value of an old-growth forest to the total board feet of timber, then translate that into dollar equivalents at present market value. For in this unprecedented journey where old maps can only lead us to previous destinations, returning us to where we have been, we must fearlessly throw such outdated charts into the evolutionary Fire as we learn to navigate by a truer body-sense, practicing a more holistic round-world economics that reintegrates ecology into the equation; revaluing the forest not only as a timber reserve but as an oxygen-creator, soil-builder, erosion-preventer, stream and watershed-protector, wildlife habitat, medicinal plant provider, preserve for beauty and solitude, matrix for genetic diversity and source of natural wonder.

For how can we continue to live by these crude mental maps and math which convert such priceless qualities and resources to dollar signs? How can we continue to calculate the real net cost of cutting down a forest in such myopic mercenary terms, religiously following such Pavlovian patterning which, this Agenda believes, not only places life at the service of business but at the service of death?

A Graduated Trans-Species Shift
from Dollars to Sense

Working through addictions, whether individual or societal, demands extraordinary endurance, perseverance and mutual support. While we are under their spell, they distort our sense of time and destroy our will, hooking us on instant gratification, running our lives through a paranoid filter that lives from fix to fix. In the case of money, then, the movement toward post-monetization, like all drug rehab programs, involves a conscious series of steps moving us gradually but methodically off the dependency; in effect, wean-ing us from one system while we allow a new pattern to emerge and clarify.

Such a radical transition, then, not only involves positive, affirmative actions but appropriate "detox" processes along the way, requiring great care, discretion, fortitude and patience as we gradually build trans-species momentum. For in this "experiment in consciousness," there is no safety net other than our own sincerity and commonsense. In which case, to avoid breaking the vessel by moving too impetuously or getting pulled back into the previous pattern's undertow by moving too timidly, we must find the right balance between pushing the envelope without exceeding system-level tolerances.

I believe this turn toward a post-monetary consciousness and the larger shift it implies has already begun, is already unfolding embryonically, scattered in various seed-stages here and there, germinating, taking root even while it remains invisible, ludicrous or threatening to those still fixated or banking on the dominant illusion. These transitional manifestations have taken numerous forms, exploring and implementing more direct-value intermediaries and alternatives: experimenting with complementary currencies; creating new community-based economic initiatives, cooperatives and prototypal models of exchange as we spiral through the more modest and initially-awkward trial-and-error shifts of *H. transitionalis*. I believe, however, that these initial experiments and attempts are the forerunners of a much deeper evolutionary wave— a wave that will continue to gather conscious force, overtaking our more institutionally-rigid egoic forms as we evolve toward the more graceful, powerful and harmonious transformations of successive species; leap-frogging forward from *polaris* to *holisticus* until we arrive at the post-human stage envisioned as *Psyche materialis* for whom there is no longer division between will and realization, true need and spontaneous fulfillment.

But to get *there*, we must begin *here*. For *transitionalis*, then, this means confronting the paradigmatic resistance of the money power in its grossest, most threatened and entrenched forms; not simply addressing institutional change but the controlling egoic mindset behind those institutions; exposing the extraordinary depths to which we are hypnotized, brain-washed and programmed into a distorted reality that we blindly repeat and reconstruct at each moment. For until we deconstruct these egoic thought patterns and ideological gods that pull us like puppets on strings, calling the bluff of their default thinking, how can we hope to redefine and replace their default-patterned institutions with truer, wiser, more selflessly sustainable alternatives?

For the barrier-breakers, however, this up-stream transformation of vision, patterns and goals comes at a heavy price. For despite the do-good rhetoric that pervades our high-profile celebrity fundraisers and charitable causes, money comes far more easily to those who buy into its supremacy, who accept its sovereignty. It is highly unlikely, then, that it will willingly support or finance its own dethroning. In other words, if we are prepared to play money's game, remaining its loyal subjects, it will reward us accordingly in that subtle Faustian bargain that trades dollars for souls. On the other hand, if we dare to actually challenge the reign and cardinal rules of our monetocracies, working toward the reestablishment of truer collective values and urgently-needed alternatives in the fields of energy, environment, education and healthcare, one is left, despite New Age applications of "prosperity consciousness," competing for table scraps. (Witness our struggling non-profit organizations at the bottom of the financial food-chain.)

It is precisely this distorted priority and reward system, then, this disparity between the mega-salaries of Fortune 500 CEOs and the begging bowl of cutting-edge researchers, that we must expose and reverse; returning us to our senses; rewarding meaning rather than meaninglessness, selfless service rather than gluttony; consciously redirecting money toward the very things which challenge and transform its all-powerful addiction and lethal distortion of our lives and values. To effectuate this "conversion," however, we must begin to redefine our financial terms, reinforming meaning into our bankrupt economic vocabulary. For example, how can we go on buying into Wall Street culture's definition of "investment" which, through its dealer-user consciousness, effectively degrades the term to a speculative scheme of money-making that has more in common with gambling than value-based investments in our social and environmental well-being?

In this light, we must first address this counterfeit currency of meanings and values, breaking its egoic template rather than merely throwing out the counterfeit notes it prints. For it is this false mindset that has taken us hostage, divesting our societies of real goals, visions and direction. It is not enough, however, to simply break the mental mechanism in us and our societies that continues to crank out our forged values. We must replace that template with a truer one: redefining a truer sense of investment so that we can begin to print and imprint new meaning in matter; bringing our actions into alignment with a more progressive, postegoic perception; translating the profound principles of oneness and self-giving into real economic terms, goals, policies and directions; implementing a real reinvestment in our personal/planetary well-being.

For as we take off the blinders that have tunnel-visioned us to see the world through money, I believe we will gradually regain a lost Sense; recognizing, like recovering amnesia victims, real needs; redefining what constitutes real wealth; reclaiming our present for our future.

As a corollary to our redefinition of investment, I believe we must simultaneously redefine our concept of work, erasing the egoic connotations that reduced it to a mechanically conditioned exercise where the pay-off simply pays the bills; creatively reformulating work from a salary-motivated codependency to a consciously-chosen activity that expands and enriches us individually and collectively, within and without; turning work from drudgery to dance —to a more rhythmic and "mystic" means through which to materially discover, express and fulfill one's true self, true gift and utility in the service of a larger, more creative and creatively-joyful whole.

To effectively implement this newer, more integrated sense of work, however, we must rewrite our criteria for work and choice of work as well, reversing reference points and values from outer to inner: i.e., from whatever happens to be available or pays the best wages to what would actually best serve our true socio-environmental needs and, at the same time, best express our true inner net worth; in effect, retrofitting our production-line economic models, systems, priorities and thinking, designing jobs to fit people and meet authentic needs rather than arbitrarily molding people into jobs run by the engine of advertising.

Following this new orientation, education is rescued from its present subservience to business, returned to its true mission as an instrument for the pursuit of knowledge and culture. For once education reassumes its rightful role as leader and visionary rather than indentured servant to the mercantile class, its systematic quest for knowledge becomes the collective mechanism not only to illumine and awaken the individual's deeper potentials and skills but to bring a more holistic approach, value system and understanding of how the individual can best contribute her gift to the utility, integration and well-being of the whole. In this creative scenario, then, education collaborates with work, liberating and inspiring it into a source of freedom rather than burden: into a self-expression that receives more energy than it expends, releasing a joy that one can only know through the divine dynamic of true self-giving.

$$\xi$$

If this perspective still appears too utopian, reality-check the present tradeoff: How much of our stress-related neuroses, criminal and sociopathic behavior can be traced to uneducated and un-fulfilled human potentials, soulless employment just to pay the bills, misemployment of inner gifts and possibilities, or unemploy-ment for those who simply don't fit in? And how much does this "cost" each of us and our societies every day in terms of despair, disease, misapplication of energies, crime and other forms of self-destruction? These are critical questions that deserve legitimate re-search. However, with *egoicus* still primarily in charge of curricula, which schools of economy, research institutes or investment houses are actually willing to factor such questions and costs into their syl-labi and portfolios? The Emperor, we must remember, is the last one to admit he has no clothes, despite the designer price-tag.

If we would free ourselves, then, from our egoic blinders, letting ourselves begin to breathe a more possible and positive air, it is not folly but wisdom to visualize a society that revalues true net worth and potential; producing things based on real needs rather than inflated ones; where our advertising, media and cyber-systems are placed at the service of education, research and information rather than greed, escapism and salesmanship; where marketing skills presently subverted by ignorant and lethally-misguided notions of profit would be used to "sell" us into a truer direction for the well-being of all; where ad-men would employ the same seductive skills of the trade turned toward the light, pointing us toward a progress no longer modeled upon a world sliced up into so many compet-ing fragments; leading us toward a junkmail-free world where money-related crime became an anachronism and lawsuit-less lawyers were free to focus on issues of conscience and social justice.

Let us begin, then, to creatively and self-empoweringly visualize this Society as a first practical step towards its realization; beginning to re-dream our truths; daring to propose (as the following chapter, "Evolutionary Activism," intends to explore) an economy where we are guided by the will, wit and wisdom of our child-warrior selves rather than the cowardice and blindness that presently governs our governments and board-rooms; no longer servicing our debts, feeding the demand of our dominant hardcore habits, by cannibalizing our social, educational environmental and health-care budgets; freeing doctors and other related professionals to get on with their "real business," motivated solely by the will to heal and serve their highest truth rather than by the more mercenary dictates of HMOs, the cross-expectations of financial reward or the pressing repayment of astronomical school loans.

For once we have visualized such a society and the utter sensibility of it relative to the present madness we passively or actively sustain and support, we *can* begin to act upon that vision; gradually, persistently bringing outer realities into correspondence with it, confident somehow that we will realize our goals, despite present appearances to the contrary, because we begin to feel and *know* its evolutionary truth and inevitability; reminding ourselves that all evolutionary breakthroughs are heretical to the prevailing paradigm, just as the notion that the earth was round or humans evolved from apes was once dismissed as lunacy or heresy.

For what *is* true wealth, after all, if not a *well-being* that goes to the very heart of who we are and what we can become individually and together? And how can we ever get there as a species until we find the courage to admit what we all know in our hearts?—saying aloud what the child in us has never forgotten despite the intimidation of our fears and peers: That beneath the Emperor's egoic armor, he is naked!

Rather than continuing to cover up this fact, then, hiding our emptiness from ourselves at any cost, why not just drop the unbearable weight of our nothingness and fill its void with a truer value?—revaluing ourselves and Nature on a more divine scale than dollars, re-entrusting power to leaders and elders whose vision is no longer leased to lobbyists or soulless transnationals, re-empowering ourselves in the process to actually take charge of our lives.

For in this simplest gesture, I believe we begin to forge a truly trustworthy humanity, creating through that conscious vehicle a Trust for the Earth: An unprecedented evolutionary Trust where the primitive egoic instincts to own and control mature and transform into the will to steward and share. Where selflessness replaces selfishness as the means toward Self-fulfillment in a wealth that paradoxically grows by self-giving.

A Trust for the Earth founded on a genuine identity with and compassion for all, deeded in the knowledge that the well-being of the individual and the whole are indivisibly one.

NINE

EVOLUTIONARY ACTIVISM

A Trust for the Earth begins by rebuilding a trust with and within our selves; expanding that trust from body to body, cell to cell, person to planet; forging in the process the missing links in a conscious Trust that spans not only in space but time; bringing together present and future selves in a vast inter-species collaboration.

Such a Trust is rooted in an unshakeable faith and commitment. A commitment willing to stand up not only for social, political, economic and environmental justice, but for an *integral* justice that springs from a core change of consciousness at the very roots of our species. A core change not simply of a revolutionary but evolutionary nature; fronting not only our cultural and institutional machinery but the very way of knowing, seeing and being that guards and governs that machinery; growing into a consciousness that no longer plays by the egoic rules of divide and conquer, no longer lives by the empiric laws of division; healing us of the illusion that would simply replace one regime, one machine, with another while still leaving the gene, the program, the blind I that spins and replicates the distortion, intact.

This change of consciousness, I believe, is leveraged from within by an activism far more radical than any of its revolutionary human spin-offs. For it is, as this millennial Agenda has previously referenced it, an *evolutionary* activism, poised and primed toward nothing less than the integral overthrow of the egoic Empire, humbling the mechanism of Mind to a subordinate and supportive role through the infusion of a new *supra*mental principle of Being into Matter and material processes.

Motivated by an evolutionary Force far more resolute, inspired and magnetizing than mere moral or political idealism, this integral activism effectively reunites the once-polarized paths of peace and power; invoking an invincible evolutionary dynamic that acts directly, vibrationally upon the body, cellular and terrestrial; not simply overpowering from without but setting up a resonance that "agitates" the "particles" of consciousness in the surrounding material field. In effect, this "agitation" (imaged here in the less-pejorative language of physics rather than politics) awakens and quickens that same power locked within each crystallized form; setting in motion the consciousness equivalent of a nuclear chain reaction; catalyzing and releasing this truer power and potential lying dormant (i.e., unconscious or half-conscious) within each being and form; freeing that power to consciously *trans*form the instrumental vessels it inhabits; out-sustaining the counter-reactive resistances through an inexorable takeover from within.

In this context, the role of the evolutionary activist is one of midwifing our metamorphosis. While working, then, through practical fields, outer processes and domains that match the unique skills, experience and expertise of the activist, the inner process and inner action remains the same. In other words, whether the "agent" is operating in the environmental, socio-economic, scientific, artistic, cultural or entrepreneurial domains, or in some creative combination of them, these outer fields are simply channels through which one invites and infuses a new evolutionary principle into Matter; in effect, "radioactivating" the particular field through which one acts; shaking it (i.e., vibrating it at an accelerated rate) from its present status quo trance; provoking in the most positive and profound sense a mutation of consciousness.

ξ

Transcribed through the metaphor of healing and health, the role of the evolutionary activist is to become a carrier for a new, positive contagion; inoculating present with future to counter the negatively-inherited contagion of viral programs that plague our planetary atmosphere and keep us locked in our past. For with each unconscious mental breath, we unwittingly breathe in these lethal viruses of doubt, fear and self-defeatism; catching and transmitting them; reinfecting one another; providing them a "host" in which they can proliferate into ever-more-clever, ego-resistant strains that weaken and wear away our psycho-social immune systems through their constant negative bombardment until we finally succumb to hopelessness and despair. Until we effectively give up and give in to the prevailing pattern.

In addition to playing the role of catalytic agent for mutational change, then, through specific fields of action, the evolutionary activist simultaneously recognizes the urgent and essential need to bring individuals together; coalescing them out of their isolation into larger, more creative context, contact and concert with one another. For by generating these expanding embryonic communities, collective support networks and organizations, releasing divided and alienated energy back into more unified, concerted and integrally-empowered forms, we

- provide more holistic focal-points to exponentially magnify the effectiveness and potential of isolated individuals;
- establish the human equivalent of "mutational field generators" through these emergent seed-communities and "centers of evolutionary activism";
- build up positive psycho-social energy fields and species-level immune systems to withstand the debilitating negativity and still-dominant default sense of impossibility which our sense of separateness, alienation and alone-ness fosters.

After all, mutational change and evolutionary transformation are processes that not only impact the individual but encompass larger and larger wholes, operating horizontally through expansion and embrace as well as vertically through the "descent" of a heightened awareness, vision and power. In any case, if we are to embody (as this work has already premised) our goals in the very means, methods and processes to realize them; and if wholeness and integrality are essential evolutionary goals, how can we ever truly achieve or manifest them in isolation, regardless of our inner realizations? While it may be necessary at synaptic moments in our personal development, then, to enter the solitude of what we call spiritual retreat in order to incubate and consolidate vertical breakthroughs, these are interim phases, breathing in before breathing out; regathering, reintegrating and preparing ourselves for future plunges back into the surrounding collective field which we recognize as our larger contextual self.

It is in this sense, as we shall continue to explore, that community and community-based action is critical to the fulfillment of our evolutionary goals and transitional roles as a species; moving us in humble, practical yet unstoppable steps toward a trans-humanity that begins to operate from the same inter-supportiveness that we presently reserve for nuclear families; in effect, expanding the identity and cell wall of the nuclear family to the circumference of humanity and all the other life forms with whom we share terrestrial existence; materially recentering and reorienting our lives around the nucleus of a truer reality and reference-point oneness.

The Responsibility of Oneness

Everything we consume and, through that consumption, support or export as a global economic pattern, has direct consequences for our planet: for our reserves of natural resources and carbon-based fuels; for our air and water quality; for the fluctuations of our temperature, climate and biospheric thermostat; in fact, for the entire terrestrial web of life that shares this interwoven existence with us. In which case, operating from the biological and ecological premise that all life *is* one, we must begin to *act like it*, moving from rhetoric to reality, coming into alignment with facts that our minds still relegate to abstract or optional ideals. In other words, we must begin to accept the responsibility of actually *living* that oneness.

This responsibility is not simply motivated by a deeper moral sense and obligation. For as we have noted, if morality, religious ethics and ideals could transform us, we would have changed long ago. We know, for example, that war makes no sense as a way to resolve conflicts, in fact, is a contradiction in terms; yet we continue as a species to pursue it as a primary nation-state strategy. In fact, pursue it with gusto, hyper-industrialized countries marketing it as big business, rich states and poor alike often allocating more money to defense budgets than all of their social, healthcare, educational, cultural and scientific research programs combined.

How is this possible? Where is the correspondence with our so-called "civilized" values?

Or is the truth of the matter that we are essentially a conflicted species whose professed inner values often have little or no say in our preordained egoic priorities and outer behaviors? And that consequently, we only change when the pain of present habit-patterns becomes unbearable?—when the threat is mortal, not moral, leaving us with only two options: Death or change? (And even then, there are die-hards who would rather go down with the ship, bringing everyone down with them rather than surrender ego, admit ignorance and change course.)

This imperative need, then, for us to accept specie-level responsibility for our oneness is no longer just a matter of idealism but rather of pragmatic evolutionary realism; recognizing in fact that every act, every gesture that equates survival with competition—that supports our division and *dis*connection, in other words, *our un-oneness*—unconsciously leads us toward further pain, trauma, *dis*integration and death: A scenario, ironically, in which only the threat of extinction itself carries sufficient force to change us, the fear of death becoming our last-resort insurance policy and ultimate motivator for us to *live* our oneness.

In this light, then, let us examine the implications of our lifestyles—of what we eat, drive and buy—in order to distinguish which are legitimate lifestyles and which, in fact, are devolutionary "deathstyles"; re-establishing the critical connections between the micro and macro: Between the cars we choose or the foods we crave and the depletion of our planetary resources, the fragmentation of our ozone layer, the poisoning of our oceans, soils and cities. In other words, the direct body-link between us and the biosphere we cannot live without.

To begin this inquiry into present consumer patterns and priorities, it is critical at the outset to distinguish between legitimate needs and egoic cravings that have passed themselves off as needs. For it is this blind-I confusion—creating an economy and reality designed to service and satisfy an ego which, by virtue of its bottomless pit, can never be satisfied—that, I believe, sets up our core conflict with Nature and ourselves: A conflict sanctioned and justified by a biblical fundamentalism that cut Matter from Spirit, effectively placing Her at the disposal of a dwarf lord who, governed by a half-evolved sensory perception which splits oneness through a mental prism, has lost sight of the fact that She is his own outwardly-manifest self.

With this perspective, then, as a vantage point, let us start with the question of food. Is it just a matter of taste? nutrition? If we can afford it, shouldn't we be free to choose what we wish to eat? After all, as the ego would have us believe, it is *our* body, isn't it?

Or is it? For if we step back from our egoic default relationship with and perception of our bodies, is what we call *our* body really "ours," isolated from "others" as our outer senses continue to reinforce? Or is it more accurate to see it as a cell in a vast interconnected terrestrial organism that in fact belongs to none of us separately yet all of us together? In which case, everything we do, think or say not only effects us locally but, in degrees, the entire field of which we are a part. And while the consequences of a single individual's actions on the planet may be negligible (though there are notable exceptions), just as the impact of a single cell on the body may hardly register in its general functioning, if we multiply that cellular behavior a billion-fold, its effects may be disastrous (or transformative, as the case may be).

This archaic ego-sense, then, that believes it should be free to do as it likes, as if it's operating in a vacuum, finds its parallel blindspot in the impact of second-hand smoke, which eventually, as we have learned, can be just as deadly as first-hand. Just as the toxins with which a farmer dusts *his* fields don't recognize the "private property" boundary markers and fencelines, infiltrating *our* water tables, bleeding into *our* air and streams in a closed loop in which we all live downstream and downwind. As we move into the twenty-first century, then, we must expand our very concept of "ours," widening it to a far more inclusive, comprehensive and post-proprietary sense of self-identity; readapting through that larger identity our present notions of freedom and rights to a less privatized, less fragmented reality; reframing rights in the context of responsibilities; reframing responsibilities in the context that we are one inextricably-united body: A body-reality in which none of us is truly free until all of us is free.

Returning to the question of food, then, how much do our food choices not only impact our individual body-health and consciousness but the state of our shared planetary body? And can we begin to think in terms of an evolutionary or trans-species diet?

Breaking these generic questions down into more specific ones, how does vegetarianism, for example, differ from a meat-based diet in terms of terrestrial impact? And has the motivation for vegetarianism shifted under the present stress of evolutionary circumstances, globalized awareness and economic globalization? For, historically speaking, vegetarianism as a voluntary dietary choice originally evolved out of ethical concerns for sentient animals, hygiene issues, or some alchemic or shamanic association between food sources and states of consciousness.[1]

Though these motivations or some combination of them still influence the turn toward vegetarianism, I believe new evolutionary factors have entered into the equation, moving vegetarianism from a fringe or cult diet to a more mainstream alternative. These new factors and awarenesses include a concern for the massive infusion of hormones and antibiotics pumped into our herds to promote a higher output of assembly-line beef, the cholesterol effect of red meat on heart and brain function, and the enhanced knowledge of the chemical relationship between nutrients and body-mind states. But in addition to these more personalized health and body-mind connections which have begun to inform our dietary choices, I believe there is another emergent level of consciousness, operating from a deeper dimension of person-planet oneness, that has intervened, influencing not only the trend toward vegetarianism but towards organic foods.

For vegetarianism alone no longer assures us a "purer" diet, free

---

1. For example, in India's Hindu traditions, foods, thoughts and activities are categorized in three primary modes as: *sattvic* (light-fed and light-enhancing), *rajasic* (vitally energizing and impassioning) or *tamasic* (contributing to lethargy, inertia and obscurity). In terms of food vis-à-vis consciousness, then, *tamasic* would be the least "spiritual" choice.

from harmful chemical residues (whose long-term effects have yet to be fully monitored or disclosed) in the things we eat, the milk we drink and feed our children. Nor does it factor in the over-refinement (i.e., white sugar and flour) or over-processing of foods which, at a certain point, if one reads the labels, resemble synthetic pseudo-foods. Whereas the turn toward organics, as we shall explore, points directly toward the healing, wholing and re-identification of individual and planetary health.

The conscious return to organic agriculture is a movement whose magnitude touches far more than food. For it goes to the very roots of our relationship with the earth, addressing not simply a change of systems but of systems thinking, reestablishing the link which has been lost as agri*culture* turned with frightening success into agri*business*.

While mid-twentieth century versions of this conversion toward agribusiness—notably the export of the "green revolution"—may have provided a critical short-term response to famines and depleted grain reserves in third world countries, its symptomatic approach still missed the deeper underlying causes of human impoverishment which, I believe, lies in a hunger of the heart: in human un-oneness and its subsequent fragmentation into egoic "haves" and "have-nots." In fact, in many ways, this reflex reliance upon technologies as a panacea not only diverts attention from truly resolving matters at the core but actually compounds the problem, creating unforeseen yet far more life-threatening complications in the process. Which is what happens when humans tinker with Nature *before* working out the egoic obscurities and overlays that motivate, guide and govern *human* nature.

For by cornering ourselves into a food and agricultural pattern that reinforced our dependency more and more heavily upon chemical fertilizers, pesticides, bio-tech processes and processing to increase yield, quantity, appearance and marketability, we polluted and toxified our planet as a by-product; by surrendering biological, sociological and ethical decisionmaking to ad execs, we laid claim to the very genetic codes of the cell, modifying and patenting seed genetics as if they were "intellectual property," placing science at the service of salesmen; by unleashing the forces of finance to drive the engine of farming, trying to improve upon or outsmart Nature's ecological and soil-building processes by inorganic "accelerants," we not only reduced soil from a living organism to a mechanized production factory but we degraded our farm workers as well, exposing them to hazardous substances and harsh working conditions for subsistence wages, letting our stomachs run our hearts rather than the other way round.

It is this far deeper disconnection, then, that organic farming addresses, working from the ground up to humbly heal an un-oneness that still governs our macro-policymaking. For by consciously changing our choice of food, moving not merely from meat-based to vegetarian but to organically-grown, we not only cultivate a more conscious, pro-evolutionary diet but implement a more pro-evolutionary relationship with earth and our fellow humanity.

Returning to the more generic question of animal versus plant-based food sources, there is another implication and level of impact in such a shift that should not be overlooked. This concerns the effect that meat-based diets have on land and resource use patterns. In other words, if we no longer depended upon livestock as our culture's primary protein source, if we systematically reduced and eventually replaced meat-based with vegetable-based proteins (such as we are seeing in the trend toward soy and tofu alternatives) as part of a larger trans-species shift, we would dramatically reverse the present red-line depletion of natural resources that our massive herds consume, devastate or deforest.

It is, after all, a far more ecologically-efficient use of land, water and energy to extract essential nutrients directly from plants such as soy rather than by reprocessing photosynthesized food through the additional intermediary of livestock. For through this intermediary, we not only create an enormous secondary step that consumes exponential quantities of natural resources simply to convert already-edible vegetable matter into the more complex animal form of meat; but we increase through the subsequent "manufacturing" process the background level of sentient species trauma, suffering and pain. In addition, the enormous quantity of methane gas generated by our terrestrial herds significantly contributes to green house gases and global warming.

From this more conscious eco-perspective, then, we begin to understand just how much leverage our fork and spoon exerts. For the very health and sustainability of our planet is directly linked to what we put on our plate—to our food choices and the web of industries, by-products and socio-economic patterns we consciously or unconsciously support by those choices. If we would change these patterns, then, we must be willing to confront their gravity at the personal level. For collective change humbly begins at home. This means changing what's on *our* plate, *our* lifestyle menu, without waiting for the permission or legislation of others.

Such repatterning shifts, as this Agenda has already developed in principle, inevitably involve degrees of personal sacrifice, in this case, forgoing some of our most-cherished though least-enlightened food-habits. Looked at, however, from a psychological perspective, this, after all, is precisely what it means to mutate at the micro-level, confronting and transforming the addicted, Pavlovian-conditioned parts of our nature that keep us locked in the gravity of past patterns and behaviors.

For how else shall we develop and express a truer free will and inner self-mastery if we are not willing to surrender devolutionary habits, diets and cravings, mental, emotional and physical? If we are not willing to opt for those that reflect our deeper commitment to oneness, cultivating in the process a more conscious "taste" for oneness? For it is this conscious choice and commitment that will not only lead us to newer, consciousness-based evolutionary forms of nutrition, but—as part of a larger "conspiracy" and more integral transformative process—to the evolution of new bodily and organic functions: changing both what we eat as well as the way we metabolize it; adapting and incorporating more enlightened land use patterns to grow "lighter" foods, which in turn impact not only our terrestrial body but our personalized cellular and organic evolution; prompting more transparent ways to assimilate and convert these lighter, more consciously-grown nutrients into more conscious forms of energy and matter.

Applying this same transformational grass-roots approach, principle and perspective to the issue of fuels (after all, the energy sources that drive the engines of our societies are simply mechanical macro-versions of metabolizing what humans call food), what is the terrestrial impact of our present choice of cars, transportation and technologies and the fuel-forms that run them? And is there an impact parallel between the reliance on livestock as a primary food source and carbon-based fossil fuels as a primary energy source?

In other words, is an economy run primarily on oil, coal and natural gas—on fossil fuels formed over millions of years through the decomposition of once-living matter—an efficient, reliable, sustainable and clean-burning system? Is it a system powered by our past or our future: By entrenched societal habit-patterns, fossilized ways of thinking and being, carefully guarded by commercial and institutional interests that would keep us addicted to those fossil-fueled patterns and dependencies? Or by our ingenuity and imagination as a species to design and create new, non-polluting, renewable forms of energy and appropriate technologies that reflect the eco-genius, elegance and simplicity of Nature's photosynthetic, alchemical and synergistic processes?

These questions, I believe, help us more consciously clarify the larger choices before us, establishing an evolutionary reference point and guideline for species-level decisionmaking with regard to cars, transportation infrastructure and technologies. For like food and agriculture, our vehicles are largely designed, driven and marketed by money motives; fixating us on a menu that highlights looks, sexiness, luxury and mass rather than critical factors such as fuel-efficiency and clean alternatives to the internal combustion engine; appealing to egoic values and choices in the same way that we have addicted ourselves to the taste for tastes that are killing us, trading off nutrition and health for fast-food cravings.

Pursuing this analogy between food, fuel and cars, we begin to see just how interrelated and interwoven all of these issues actually are; waking up to the evolutionary reality that we cannot truly solve any of them until we resolve all of them as a whole. In other words, until we solve *us*, recognizing finally, as we look at ourselves and our planet in a reality-mirror no longer seen through a blind I, the integral implications and responsibilities of living our oneness.

With regard to our choice of cars, then, and the fuels that run them, us and our industries, we can no longer simply choose according to our myopic, egoic "our," buying whatever we like just because we have the money. For it is precisely this illusory sense of separateness and un-oneness, supported by the false power that money arbitrarily confers upon its partisans, which is killing us, particularly now at this accelerated evolutionary moment where every decision we make has increasingly more direct biofeedback consequences for us all.

What good is it, after all, to attend conferences or workshops on global warming, the control of CO_2 emissions or renewable energy systems, grasping the conceptual level of the problem, if we drive to those meetings in gas-guzzling dinosaurs? What good is it to talk about rainforest preservation and the protection of species diversity that those rainforests support if we continue to buy into fast-food patterns that convert those ancient forest habitats into fodderlands for hamburgers? What good is it to petition congressional representatives to save Arctic wildernesses from being bidded out to oil profiteers while we continue to support gluttonous fossil-fuel-based lifestyles, products, industries and economics, consuming and demanding more and more of the earth's resources as if, as Schumacher pointed out, we were drawing from interest rather than our planet's irreplaceable capital reserves?

In fact, how many wildernesses and rainforests could we save if we simply consumed less, increased the fuel efficiency of our vehicles, homes and businesses? How much sanity might we restore to our lives, lifestyles, cities and countrysides if we prioritized new "lighter" forms of transportation and mass transit, which in turn, as with more enlightened foods, led to new adaptive designs for the evolution of our societal macro-bodies based on the reality of our oneness? For such a shift in perspective, value and choices, I believe, will have a chain-reaction effect, returning our roads, highway systems and traffic patterns to a more human scale; promoting in the process a more viable, integrated sense of Community and communication between where we live and where we work; creating more vibrant, interactive neighborhoods that at the same time encourage alternatives such as biking and walking as we reduce the distances between ourselves, our lives, our work and our joy; reviving the healthy use of our bodies that, particularly in the western world, have atrophied, succumbing to a debilitating over-mentalization as we buffered ourselves further and further behind mind-constructed intermediaries and codependencies, trading off living realities for virtual ones.

§

While it is critical for us, then, at this evolutionary turning point to speak up for our beliefs, calling the bluff of our apathy, speaking up in the face of injustice for those of us who do not have a voice, nevertheless, what we actually *do* and *buy* speaks more loudly than what we say. For it is in these humble actions that we actually heal our default-patterned disconnections and contradictions—that we actually begin to practice an evolutionary activism, living our oneness, following a body sense that sees directly: distinguishing real values from egoic counterfeits; converting a value-blind economic apparatus to a conscious, creative eco-system; putting our money not only where our mouth is but where our heart is; learning to love in actions, not just the passing lip-service passion of words; reclaiming down to the most mundane details our human responsibility in the evolutionary scheme of things. The buck, after all, starts and stops here, with each of us and our personal domestic patterns.

Cutting to the Evolutionary Chase

From this evolutionary perspective of converging personal-planetary oneness, then, using Matter as an unbiased mirror to reflect the blindspots and contradictions we miss or avoid seeing in ourselves, we rediscover our own leverage in the equation: A leverage that, if we join together, can pry us forward into a new species. This formidable civilizational shift begins, however, at the beginning, bringing it all back home, by

- re-examining our own personal lifestyles and consumer patterns: what we eat, drive, crave and buy (in other words, our body-habits);
- and then bringing those body-habits into alignment with our inner vision and core values, letting an enlightened body-consciousness guide and inform our once-imperial mental consciousness, freeing us from the subservience to

Mind's arbitrary overlays and biases, seeing what needs to be done and simply doing it, placing more attention on resolving our own contradictions, insincerities and hypocrisies before trying to convert others.

For it is here, in the least exotic, most humbling and mundane, that we find out what we are really made of: How much we are willing to *live* and *become* the changes we would see in the world; fronting and conquering that second-nature egoic reflex in us to transfer blame or project onto others the changes too painful to make in oneself; accepting our individualized portion and co-responsibility for the unconsciousness we unwittingly contribute to the collective state of affairs; taking on our own unique share of the terrestrial patterns that must change along with our corresponding share of the transformational pain involved in changing those patterns.

For I believe it is in this personal gear-shifting that we discover the true evolutionary meaning behind the concept of sacrifice; translating in secular terms the daily, anonymous yet profoundly-heroic sacrifice of the ego at the altar of one's true self, one's true values; transforming ourselves invisibly and incrementally at each metamorphic moment until we finally overtake our surface selves and scripts from within, emerging from the chrysalis as someone else.

For even our smallest patterns—the micro-gears and orbits in which our personal stories turn—are meshed into larger commercial, cultural and morphogenetic gears and cycles, locking us into the unconscious mechanism of institutional as well as pre-human genetic patterns and programs. In which case, for us to actually shift personal gears, we must be willing to consciously front the habitual devolutionary momentum of Time itself, bearing the egoic friction, resistance and consequent pain of gears grinding as we disengage from the clock-work machinery that presently drives human and pre-human consciousness—as micro-gears dare to exert their free will against macro-determinisms, defying the mechanical direction of countless millennia cogged together into the tightly-meshed appearance of inevitability and law, breaking free from the gravity of our species-level resignation and refrain of "this is the way it is and always will be," shattering the egoic mirror of our un-oneness to see and re-become the whole that we are.

To effectuate this evolutionary joint venture, however, consolidating individual change into workable collective forms, policies, directions and plans, I believe it is helpful to provide ourselves collective targets to focus our breakthrough energies and aspirations; giving form and direction to constructively channel what might otherwise remain a dispersed sum of individual efforts rather than a self-synergizing whole; providing us focal-point steps to lever us from the death-grip of *egoicus*; in effect, winging it, improvising it as we go along, catching the notes of a new song whose words are yet to be written; giving ourselves permission to do what has never been done rather than talking ourselves out of it simply *because* it has never been done.

Let us begin, then, to propose some twenty-first century strategies for change, allowing ourselves the liberty to consider them from the perspective of an evolutionary commonsense rather than the kneejerk cynicism that would dismiss them as the stuff of fairy tales. For in this evolutionary journey of Consciousness, it is precisely our species' transitional role to turn fairy tales true, living out our highest possibilities rather than fighting to uphold and preserve the chains that imprison us in our slavish patterns and the dungeon mentalities that guard them. Beware, then, of that little voice inside our heads that instinctively laughs at the folly of such foolhardy proposals. For behind the laugh is a nervousness that belies its posturing.

Onward, then, into our Adventure, exploring the unknown as our own future Self...

Getting Our Act Together:
Strategies for the Twenty-First Century

To consciously unblock our collective body from a constriction that presently obstructs the flow of individual and societal evolution, the evolutionary activist must play the role of cultural acupuncturist, releasing pent-up, stagnating and self-destructive energies and values. The application of this healing modality at the macro-system level, I believe, involves the release of key corporate meridians and acupuncture points presently dammed by the egoic forces of media and money. In other words, liberating

- the means of communicating ideas at the cultural and global level that, at present, influence what we think, want and buy, holding the power to perpetuate status-quo paradigms (or inject new ones); and
- the means of keeping personal and collective values under the control of a commercialized, competitive and divisive mindset that reduces social, ethical and environmental priorities to financial decision-making.

In this context, approaching our critical planetary urgencies as the direct biofeedback of evolutionary patterns that have outlived their utility (i.e., are unsustainable); and consequently, waking up to the fact that if we continue to passively follow them like lemmings, they will drag us over the evolutionary cliff, this Agenda proposes:

- The progressive elimination of money as a measure of value.
- The transformation of the media as a tool of communication.

While intimidating, even blasphemous in their starkness as bullet points, I believe these are legitimate millennial goals and undertakings for a trans-humanity. For if we get beyond our initial intimidation and second thoughts—getting past the abruptness that condenses into two terse phrases a challenge that openly contests the authority of the Goliath that has governed us for centuries, conditioning us to assume that we cannot live without him—we can actually begin to devise successful metamorphic strategies; breaking down these Herculean tasks into more manageable steps and stages; avoiding the polarizing egoic tendency to *either* take them on all at once *or* not at all; consciously carrying them out in the expanded time-spirit, patience and perseverance of an applied evolutionary research.

Toward these goals and societal realizations, then, I propose the following programs and applied research projects in the field of socio-economic transformation, inviting our collective genius as a species to take up these challenges (as well as conceive and conspire others that they may catalyze) as part of a broader species-level curriculum in an Evolutionary Agenda for the Third Millennium:

Investing in the Twenty-first Century:
A New World Stock Exchange

To provide a larger transitional context from which to begin pulling together diverse and dispersed economic experiments, creating a new collective vehicle through which to practice a truer form of Investment than our presently-bankrupted Wall Street versions, I propose the creation of a New World Stock Exchange.

This proposal is based upon the urgent need not only to visualize but evolve a sustainable alternative to our Old World stock markets and the entrenched patterns which govern them; providing our species a *real* choice rather than simply forcing us to choose from an existing menu whose options, for the most part, only differ in appearance; offering ourselves a whole new direction and incentive for *real* investment in our future rather than the devolutionary perpetuation of our past.

For the founding of a New World Stock Exchange would create

a conscious vehicle and vessel for another kind of corporation and share-holder participation; inviting entrepreneurs and corporate visionaries who recognize the distinction between true and false profits—between genuine investment in our socio-environmental well-being and speculative ventures solely for money-making—to clearly distinguish themselves in a new category; joining together in a powerful collaboration of interests that place business at the service of real planetary needs, priorities and possibilities; demonstrating a new approach to globalization, defining our oneness not through a mercantile concept of world trade that effectively trades our world away for money, but through a symbiotic process and mutuality that re-prioritizes authentic human, natural and cultural values.

This New World Stock Market, chartered and monitored to assure that member companies honor their commitments (in the same way that one oversees and certifies organically-grown from conventional), then, would not only provide a direct alternative choice for those of us who wish to effectively invest in our future; but it would turn consumers into creators, reviving old money into new; encouraging old world ventures to *evolutionize*, transferring their priorities and capital assets to the production of more relevant value, goods and services for the true benefit of all.

The proposal of an alternative stock market, rather than merely overthrowing existing trade set-ups, is an attempt to create a transitional vehicle for the practice of a new macro-economics. Because, as we have seen through the metaphor of addictions, dramatically cutting from established patterns risks the jarring dislocation and trauma of withdrawal; missing the steps to wean us gradually through interim forms that constructively channel the energy unleashed. Rather than merely choosing, then, between the extremes of leaving status quo forces in place or rejecting them completely, or the compromise attempt to infuse present market set-ups with new ventures, this approach seeks to create a whole new vessel. For such a new vessel not only avoids the polarizing all-or-none tendencies of egoic problem-solving, but the compromise as well that would risk pouring new wine into old skins, effectively diluting, corrupting and eventually overpowering such trickle-in ventures under the gravitational weight and greed-based motivations imprinted in the very walls of Wall Street and the old boys empire that runs it.

In this scenario, then, the initial start-up concept behind a New World Stock Exchange would be an alliance of unique yet integrated and interrelated ventures and investors whose common goal was the re-creation of core values in a living system; predicated on a vision that no longer split economic from ecologic priorities; reuniting the two in their common root prefix, *eco*, derived from the Greek *oîko(s)*, meaning "house": In other words, the management of our house, our shared terrestrial home, based on the study, understanding and respect of its living systems.

Such a joint venture, I believe, would not only provide a clearly-distinguished channel for consumers, investors and enterprises already aligned with the principles, practices and values of such a holistically-conceived stock market; but could jump-start a whole new wave of "capital" initiatives and investments in research, development, promotion and mainstreaming of:

> Organic food industries and agriculture; sustainably certified wood products, ecosystem-guided forest management practices, forest stewardship jobs and job-training; renewable, non-polluting energy technologies (solar, wind, biogas, fuel cell, etc.), consumer waste and wastewater recycling systems, and transportation prototypes where the attention is to conserve resources while increasing efficiency

and quality; "green" architecture, building materials and integrated systems planning, designing healthier, more energy-efficient, eco-friendly as well as attractive homes, workplaces and urban environments; holistic healthcare industries where primary emphasis is on an integrated well-being and treatment is guided by health-based rather than accountant-based principles; (fill in the blank…).

In addition to supporting these pro-evolutionary companies, services, products and processing methods, this new investment strategy would fund

- New ways to market such goods and services through the creation of ad industries mandated to inform and enlighten rather than addict and sell.
- New ways to accelerate access to information that furthers our oneness and evolutionary potential.
- Visionary planning and applied research institutes missioned to innovate, promote and map the way toward a society based on collaboration rather than competition, real rather than artificial values, true rather than fabricated needs; helping us evolve the interim social and economic steps in a direction that we discover as we go along: charting new bioregional land use and watershed policies; new cooperative-based consumer patterns that move us toward simpler, more balanced, elegant and sustainable lifestyles; returning decisionmaking to a human scale where cause and effect relationships and connections can be seen, felt and understood; reintegrating and redirecting ourselves from the competing half-truths of market or state-driven economies to holistic, community-rooted management bodies confederated within the context of a progressively evolving planetary whole.

Transforming Our Media:
Learning to Communicate with Our Future

It is virtually impossible to imagine the transformation of our societies and the re-infusion of real value into our lives, cultures and economies without a parallel transformation of the media and its power of mass communication. For a transformed media would not only complement, elucidate and accelerate emerging evolutionary processes but consciously mitigate the friction and trauma of these unfolding changes.

Such a conversion, however, as with that of the money-power, will require the ingenuity, marathonic perseverance and conviction of a true evolutionary activism. For, with the exception of Public Broadcasting, (which, in subtler ways, still remains vulnerable to commercial influence, infection and dependence), our television, film, radio, print, recording and cyber industries are run by bottomline commerce and a rating system that, for the most part, appeals to and perpetuates our culture's lowest common denominators.

(To test this hypothesis, observe from an impartial witness consciousness the fast-food, snack, car, video-game or beer commercials that bombard us. While clever in their use of special-effects technologies, they largely role-model moronic, often destructive humor, situations and personalities to sell us their products, addicting us not only to the things they sell but the abusive, dumbed-down behavior that sells them to us. Just as the canned sit-coms, soaps and formula films that they finance reinforce those same insipid and corrosive behaviors/values. The somewhat-more-sophisticated finance-directed ads, appealing to our gray-suited elites, are no less insidious, convincing us of our powerlessness to make intelligent economic decisions, keeping us addicted to pied-piper market analysts, revering corporate managers and investment houses as gods not only for our stock portfolios but our cultural priorities.)

At what point in this charade, then, do *we* actually take charge of the remote, not simply changing or muting the channel but upgrading mute to mutate, changing the default programming itself? For if we are to genuinely reorient our societies and their value systems, refocusing ourselves toward our enlightenment as a species; if we are to cultivate and heighten our aesthetic, ethical and environmental sensitivities as well as advocate and educate ourselves to the changes we must make, addressing our terrestrial urgencies and mitigating their traumas; then we must reclaim our power over a conscience-free media that presently controls us: A media that selectively determines for us what constitutes "news," filtering our access to information through the self-serving interests of the empires that own the networks, effectively keeping us mesmerized and locked into a self-perpetuating socio-economic mechanism, deadening our critical faculties through the repetitive barrage of demeaning, desensitizing, lobotomizing messages and scripts which that mechanism feeds us.

In this light, the transformation of our media is not simply a wishful dream for idealists but an inescapable step for *transitionalis*. For in terms of evolutionary as well as historical change, it represents the critical redirection of our species-level communication systems toward a communication with our future rather than past; reclaiming the means of mass communication rather than merely "killing our TVs" as the bumper stickers exhort us; effectively turning an invaluable tool and power into a positive evolutionary ally rather than simply rejecting it, leaving it to the wolves, in effect surrendering it back to *egoicus* so that he can go on mesmerizing his audiences, recloning new generations of himself, keeping us locked into our self-perpetuating individual patterns and cultural programming.

ᘓ

Like the transition, then, toward a New World Stock Exchange based on a true reinvestment in our future, this twenty-first century strategic shift in communications begins first at the conceptual level, bringing the commonsense need for a more transparent media out of the subconscious closet and into our collective thoughts, conversations, realities and awareness; channeling it from talk-ourselves-out-of-it cynicism, grin-and-bear-it complaints and frustrations to a legitimately-realistic, practical and realistically-achievable evolutionary goal.

For once we have liberated the notion of a liberated media from our egoic mind's self-defeatist conditioning, we can begin to free up our individual and species-level will to realize it; moving from the immobilizing acceptance of the way things are and, hence, must always be, to an applied evolutionary research into how they actually can and should be; reminding ourselves that, just as with money, *we* created and continue to passively condone the present communication codependency—the arrangement that left our communication systems essentially in the hands of commerce. In which case, if we did this, albeit unconsciously or half-consciously, to ourselves, then we too can rectify that arrangement, consciously readapting and progressively replacing its present control mechanism with a more enlightened one.

Communication, after all, is not a commodity for sale, no more than the oceans, the earth or its biosphere. If we accept this premise, then, it is our species-level duty to reclaim our means of communication, placing it at the service of our planetary future, our children, our truer self; working simultaneously through individual effort, risk-taking and initiative as well as collective, community and organizational-based actions as we build momentum toward critical-mass breakthroughs.

Individual effort, I believe, effectively translates through our consumer choices: i.e., through what we consciously choose to watch, read, listen to, purchase and support, paying particular attention to those things (i.e., videos and videogames) we let "babysit" our children. If the choices themselves are limited, however, then we must positively expand them rather than simply reject the negative. For the goal in communications as in evolution itself is not merely to eliminate or transcend the problem, zeroing down to a blank screen, a blank field, but to fulfill that screen, that field, with our noblest inspirations, visions and creative potentials. What, after all, is the real purpose of communications if not to more consciously express, transmit, receive and share the true joy, beauty, creative delight, self-knowledge, oneness and wonder of Being?

To effectively expand our choices, then, liberating our media (like our education) from its servitude to commerce, we must magnify individual activism a million-fold; establishing clear, identifiable goals in order to organize and focalize collective will into dynamic, community-empowered actions; daring not only to *think* Promethean thoughts but self-confidently *act* upon them; in this case, methodically working to create a new, more transparent twenty-first century network, vessel and vehicle for an emerging consciousness; rewiring our macro-communications systems and infrastructures as we rewire ourselves and our senses; discarding the remote as we reclaim a more hands-on reality, creating in the process a legitimate post-commercial alternative: A Consciousness-based Broadcasting System (See-Be-Yes) to channel new possibilities, paradigms, scripts and frequencies; mainstreaming consciousness-enhancing programming presently relegated to cable-obscurity, pockets of PBS/NPR and a handful of avant-garde stations.

To pull off such a coup, however, paralleling the foundation of an alternative New World Stock Exchange, requires extraordinary conviction, determination, ingenuity and follow-through; creating sustainable working forums to bring together the multi-band expertise of those already pushing the envelope within the communications and performing arts fields—producers, scriptwriters, actors, artists and directors, editors, journalists and marketing consultants, graphic designers, technicians and system planners—along with a broad spectrum of citizen activists, facilitators, creative visionaries and entrepreneurs in order to begin

- visualizing the content for such innovative and integrated media forms;
- configuring the technical and infrastructural needs for such a communications system;
- developing the "independent" means to fund and sustain such a post-commercial network.

In other words, setting up an applied evolutionary research to map out the actual steps to get us where we need to go, countering the formidable contraction-reflex of our egoic default No with credible studies that elevate irrational doubts to real questions. For only when we can expose and formulate hesitations and fears into responsible questions can we begin to respond to them with real answers, turning present limitations into opportunities for growth.

§

Institutions and institutional behavior, we must recognize, cycle at slower wavelengths than individuals. As a result of this more sluggish institutional consciousness and its denser egosphere, its capacity to absorb change not only proceeds at a slower rate, but, generally speaking, with far greater resistances than at the one-on-one level; tending to ignore or outlast the more isolated pinpricks of individuals or small groups; reluctantly but inevitably responding only to more sustained, broad-based collective feedback and critical mass, especially if that feedback threatens sacrosanct market share.

There are, however, notable exceptions to this corporate/state imperviousness. Witness the galvanizing impact of courageous contemporaries such as Nelson Mandela and Julia "Butterfly" Hill, willing to stand up for human rights or redwoods despite impossible odds. Or home-grown organizational trailblazers such as Rocky Mountain Institute and New Dimensions Radio. For critical mass in matters of Consciousness, we must realize, is not just measured in numbers but intensity. There is, after all, another level of Power that one activates when one follows one's truth, staying true to one's inmost soul-conviction despite the apparent impossibility of the task or the well-intentioned advice of those who would convince us to choose a safer choice. And if one perseveres in one's quest, in living out one's truth, one eventually breaks through to this other level of Power, tapping into, invoking and channeling it just as effectively in material matters as in so-called spiritual matters.

For through this humble, determined "drilling," boring through the sediment of ourselves and the bedrock of an egoic evolutionary cycle, we finally reach the Well, discovering t/here the very source and power of Evolution Herself: That all-creative Power of a Oneness that has been here all along, *inspiring, informing, empowering* all through unconscious or part-conscious intermediaries: An irresistible Power that lies at the very heart of all, waiting for us simply to call upon Her; waiting for us to consciously awaken to Her presence, and in that awakening, to release Her shining stream to deliver us; carrying us in Her swift, unerring, harmonic flow through the intermediate forms and egoic proxies that concealed and impeded Her to birth the conscious, endlessly-creative forms of OneSelf.

In this light, then, it is our trans-species role and destiny to become evolutionary activists, consciously lending ourselves to the liberation of this Power—this Power that does not belong to us yet with which we have been divinely entrusted.

TEN

OPEN-ENDED CONCLUSIONS

As trustees and stewards for this Power, accepting the responsibility of our oneness, affirming and calling in this new evolutionary principle, I believe we both fulfill and exceed our human-beingness; becoming the midwife species for our own future selves—the creative vehicles of consciousness to heal the unresolved schism between Matter and Spirit, founding in the process a living Trust for the Earth.

In fact, when one strips away all the words, theories, premises and proposals, this Agenda has simply been a provisional blueprint to move us toward this evolutionary Trust: A lever and leverage from which to begin improvising for ourselves, prying us from our shells and spells, catalyzing us from passive evolutionary bystanders toward a willed mutation of consciousness, moving us more consciously and gracefully as a species into a larger rhythm and millennial sense of time that spirals us beyond the orbit of history and historical imperatives.

In which case, the conclusions of this work remain open-ended, awaiting the link phrases, paragraphs and passages we have yet to forge and formulate together in this remarkable Story—this living, self-evolving Story where the characters themselves become conscious, beginning to rewrite the scripts as they awaken, redrafting impossibilities into luminous realities, liberating fixed laws into free-willed expressions of an ever-unfolding Truth, turning pain itself into a fiery creative force for change rather than a meaningless sentence to which we are forever condemned.

The purpose of the mutational grain of sand in the evolutionary oyster shell, after all, is not simply to suffer or merely transcend suffering in a numbing silence, but to provoke the pearl. Just as the purpose of human-beingness lies not in who or what we seem to have been but in who and what we are yet to truly become.

The angst and anguish we are experiencing at this critical evolutionary threshold, then, is actually the labor pains of a humanity in full transition, delivering itself from itself and its residual unconsciousness as it emerges toward a more self-willed, self-conscious species. It is this emergent first-phase metamorphosis, however, that fronts the greatest intensity of that pain. For its passage, we must remember, is the most wrenching and conflicted in our process of self-deliverance, when we must pass through the vortex of evolutionary and devolutionary energies polarized to their extremes, stressing system-level tolerances at the very moment when we are most vulnerable—when we are no longer this but not yet that: an amphibious, in-between species facing the perilous, unprecedented challenges of consciously emerging on a virgin shore.

Nevertheless, we continue to straggle ashore, more and more of us at each moment, struggling to find our footing and our breath as we breach the suffocating ignorance of *egoicus*; as we materialize from the mists, shaking off our amnesia, gradually recognizing ourselves and our fellow émigrés, each of us moving at our own pace and rhythm, some of us already standing, reaching forward for future selves, others of us still stumbling, brine-slick from the sea, blinded by a transparence to which our eyes and "I"s are still unaccustomed, gasping as subconscious gills transform toward light-filled lungs.

"All life," Sri Aurobindo wrote, "is yoga." If this is the case, if life herself is the field, scope and path to the Divine, then everything we do, think, feel or say, the way we walk, will or breathe, is a part and path of that integral yoga. Every challenge and obstacle, inner or outer, personal or collective, is a test or initiation: an opportunity for consciousness to learn, grow and become more conscious. Which is why we must stay alert, awake, alive to each moment, each impulse, so that we can actually *choose* rather than simply acquiesce to the dominant thought, doubt or default pattern; adapting and adjusting to each unique situation and nuance so that we do not unconsciously superimpose uni-formulas, however true in the abstract, on living realities. For by this egoic reflex to codify and sanctify evolving truths into fixed laws, we imprison ourselves in our own past truths or those of others, succumbing to the arthritic gravity that afflicts our minds long before it manifests in our bodies.

In this sense, our lives and lifestyles become the laboratory and application for an unending evolutionary research—an ever-evolving, ever-expanding yoga of Being. From this secularized spiritual perspective, then, the mortal sin is simply getting stuck, mistaking *a* truth for *The* Truth, a transit station for the destination. Because in evolutionary terms, that which does not move forward falls back, that which stands still dies, pulled down by the devolutionary undertow.

In which case, it is critical for our species to keep moving ahead, riding the crest of the evolutionary wave, applying its will to stay ahead of its gravity; in effect, learning to remain forever young, beginning first by consciously rooting out this "stuckness" within at the attitudinal level and working outward toward the body where this attitude finally crystallizes in death. For in this rigid egoic reflex—this pre-conscious tendency that desperately clings to temporal forms, identities, ways of seeing, thinking, doing and being as the ego's primitive attempt to preserve and immortalize itself—the ego ironically creates the very conditions for the death of the forms it holds hostage, preventing those forms from expanding to incarnate the larger evolutionary life forever pressing to be born.

As a species, then, we must begin to consciously expose this tiny "death," this mortality-reflex to contract; bringing light into our subconscious caves where it hides; working it courageously, methodically yet compassionately out of our systems, cultures, thought-processes and eventually bodies; recognizing the extraordinary power that this apparently innocuous instinct holds over our lives, our governments and civilizations; humbly acknowledging the extent to which this pre-rational programming determines our second-nature biases; influencing, governing and guiding our most powerful decisionmaking, plans and policies from behind the genetic veil.

For if we look beneath the posturing, sophisticated façades and intimidating overlays that armor our authority figures, beneath the wisdom of our grand counsels that decide the course of world events, there at the core lies a fear-based instinct that shrinks at the touch of the new and unknown—a fear-based bias that we, despite our denials and fist-shaking, inherited from our amoebic ancestors, rendering that same primitive, unconscious, mechanical reflex into human form where it is almost unrecognizable. Nevertheless, there it is, a tiny cowering death, afraid of light, afraid of life, afraid of love; governing our lives from the proto-cellular level where it pulses and programs us with its micro-mantra "no"; amplifying that "no" outward; resonating and metastasizing it throughout our systems.

If we are to truly respond, then, to the critical evolutionary urgencies besieging us, our planet and its biospheric integrity, we must not lose sight of where things went awry, reminding ourselves that real transformation does not await us in some far-off spiritual summits but here in the cells. While responding, then, through evolutionary triage to the life-threatening symptoms that will kill us and our fellow species if we ignore them, gaining ourselves the survival time to undertake the more profound levels of our transformation in the centuries and millennia to come, we must keep the connection between symptom and cause; pursuing the matter all the way back to the dungeon cells where the princess lies, caught in the grip of a tiny clenched fist afraid to let go, afraid to let be.

If we would free her and us, then, changing the world from inside out, changing the very sacrosanctity of death itself, we must humbly begin here in the smallest of gestures; catching that unconscious pattern in us to close, to shut down, to retreat; recognizing these primeval patterns as the blind, instinctive reaching back for a lost oneness and love that we can only recover by consciously opening and becoming; healing rather than merely numbing that unbearable core pain of separation we experienced when we first began this journey; replacing that primal genetic memory with a memory of the future.

"No clothes," the child reminds us as the dwarf emperor strides through the streets armored in his nothingness. "No clothes, *no close, open,*" the refrain echoes within, shaking the walls of the egoic empire with an irresistible childlike simplicity that disarms all resistances, inviting us forth, inviting us out, awakening that same child-flame within us all.

And in the sanctuary of our hearts, we consciously rekindle that pure-bright flame, feeding it with ourselves and our aspirations, recognizing its voice now as our own true voice—as the hero-warrior of our soul who carries the torch of an inextinguishable evolutionary Fire.

Holding that torch fearlessly before us, then, onward into our voyage of Self-discovery, setting alight the pages of an old, time-worn story as we begin the beginning of a timeless tale that finally turns true, embracing our shadows in light, igniting Love in Matter . . .

Acknowledgements

The birth of this work has been a collaborative venture, woven of many threads, past, present and future. I gratefully acknowledge those without whom it would still have remained an unmanifest possibility:

My father, Ben Lithman, whose death unexpectedly freed me from the trance of old gravities, opening me to a new life in which this manuscript could emerge; my mother, Esther, who, despite her own personal ordeals, stood steadfastly by me through critical transitions; Marjorie Avery, my guardian angel; Michael Murphy, for his creative friendship, constructive feedback and suggestions; Steven Scholl, my capable publisher and co-conspirator; Haridas (in memoriam) and Bina Chaudhuri, who opened the door to my relationship with Sri Aurobindo, the Mother and India; Wink Franklin, IONS President Emeritus, for his nobility and open-heartedness; Michael and Justine Toms, courageous communicators; Matthew Fox, for his clarity and forthrightness, cutting through the rhetoric to live out his principles in action; Barbara Marx Hubbard, fellow explorer and evolutionary comrade, who graciously took this work under her wing; the Institute of Noetic Sciences (IONS), Rajiv Malhotra and the Infinity Foundation, and Marjorie and Ogden Kellogg, for their generous support; David Brower (in memoriam), for the privilege of his fellowship and his uncompromising fight for this planet; Laurel Reuben (in memoriam), whose courage and character saw her through her own death, reminding me to accept nothing less than the truest possible.

Contributing in miscellaneous but invaluable ways, I also extend my gratitude to Faye Weisler, Laura Roe and family, Rebecca Kageyama, Lucinda Hobart (in memoriam), Frances Vaughan, Marilyn Schlitz, Deborah Miller, Robb Ollett, Huey Johnson,

Patricia Greer, Roger Toll, Julian Lines, Hilary Best, Carol Daniels, Bob Boyé, Kathy Bryon, Mindy Toth and Ed Giordano.

Finally, holding a special place in my heart, I honor my son, "Sunny", who remains my playmate, inspiration and human reference point for what truly matters, helping me to keep it simple and centered when things get too cerebral and distorted.

INDEX

ALAN SASHA LITHMAN left San Francisco for London at the close of the 1960s, hitchhiking to India to meet the Mother of the Sri Aurobindo Ashram. That meeting with her, from whom he received the name Savitra, would lead him to spend the next 21 years in the global community experiment of Auroville, India. There, he helped jumpstart the community's educational, organizational and communications systems, its liaison and exchange programs, as well as its afforestation program which eventually planted over two million trees, transforming a barren plateau back into lush tropical forests. Authoring his first book in 1980, he documented Auro-ville's pioneering development as a Trust for the Earth. Lithman returned to the States in 1990, moving to Oregon in 1992 where he authored *The Savitri Legend* (Sigo Press). A lecturer and writer, he continues to match words with actions, engaging in social, environmental and community-based initiatives for positive change. Currently involved with the Ashland Watershed Stewardship Alliance as well as organizations such as the Institute of Noetic Sciences which helped underwrite the present work, he considers himself an evolutionary activist.

ABOUT THE INSTITUTE OF NOETIC SCIENCES

The Institute of Noetic Sciences (founded 30 years ago by Apollo astronaut Edgar Mitchel) investigates consciousness (mind and spirit), and the apparent causal relationship of consciousness to the physical world. Through the frontier sciences, transformative education, and learning communities, IONS' programs and inquiries are guided by a vision in which global wisdom emerges and prevails in the 21st century. For more information, visit: www.noetic.org